UK Ninja Dual Zone Air Fryer Cookbook 2024

The Super Easy and Flavorful Ninja Air Fryer Recipes to Satisfy Your Family's Favorites | Includes Step-by-Step Instructions for Beginners

Lourdes W. Wilson

Copyright© 2023 By Lourdes W. Wilson
All Rights Reserved

This book is copyright protected. It is only for personal use.
You cannot amend, distribute, sell, use,
quote or paraphrase any part of the content within this book,
without the consent of the author or publisher.
Under no circumstances will any blame or
legal responsibility be held against the publisher,
or author, for any damages, reparation,
or monetary loss due to the information contained within this book,
either directly or indirectly.

Disclaimer Notice:
Please note the information contained within this
document is for educational and entertainment purposes only.
All effort has been executed to present accurate,
up to date, reliable, complete information.
No warranties of any kind are declared or implied.
Readers acknowledge that the author is not engaged
in the rendering of legal,
financial, medical or professional advice.
The content within this book has been derived from various sources.
Please consult a licensed professional before attempting any
techniques outlined in this book.
By reading this document,
the reader agrees that under no circumstances is the
author responsible for any losses,
direct or indirect,
that are incurred as a result of the use of the
information contained within this document, including,
but not limited to, errors, omissions, or inaccuracies.

Contents

Introduction 1
    Getting To Know Ninja Dual Zone Air Fryers 1
    Why Choose The Ninja Dual Zone (Benefits) 1
    Tips and Tricks For Using The Ninja Dual Zone Air Fryer 2
    Cleaning And Maintenance 3
    About The Recipes 4

chapter 1 Breakfast 5
    Fried Green Tomato and Pimento Cheese Grilled Cheese 5
    Air Fryer Pigs in a Blanket 5
    Fried Zucchini Sticks 5
    Air Fryer Veggie Burger 6
    Buffalo Cauliflower Pizza Bites 6
    Chicken and Waffles 6
    Air Fryer Beef Taquitos 7
    Air Fryer Empanadas 7
    Coconut Shrimp Tacos 7
    Air Fryer Chicken Quesadillas 8
    Air Fryer Taquitos 8
    Air Fryer Gourmet Grilled Cheese 8
    Crispy Fried Sweet Potato Hash Browns 8
    Air Fryer Egg and Veggie Breakfast Pockets 9
    Air-Fried Bacon-Wrapped Egg Cups 9
    Air Fryer Chili Cheese Dogs 9
    Scotch woodcock (anchovy on toast) 9
    Porridge 10
    Full English Breakfast 10
    Traditional English Breakfast 10
    Italian-Style Frittata 11
    Air Fryer Breakfast Quesadillas 11
    Air Fryer Mini Quiches 11

Chapter 2 Lunch 12
    Crispy Fried Asparagus Fries with Lemon Garlic Aioli 12
    Crispy Fried Eggplant Rollatini 12
    General Tso's Chicken 12

Air Fryer Bacon-Wrapped Jalapeños 13
Air Fryer Stuffed Peppers 13
Air Fryer Stuffed Poblano Peppers 13
Fried Zucchini Roll-Ups with Ricotta and Spinach 14
Air Fryer Chicken Cordon Bleu 14
Air Fryer Coquilles Saint-Jacques 14
Air Fryer Chicken Parmesan 15
Air Fryer Beef and Broccoli 15
Fried Chicken Parmesan Sliders 15
Crispy Fried Sweet Potato Fritters with Spicy Aioli 15
Air Fryer Beef Bourguignon Pot Pie 16
Crispy Fried Artichoke Salad with Lemon Parmesan Dressing 16
Air Fryer Beef Daube Provençal...17
Air Fryer Duck à l'Orange with Grand Marnier Sauce 17
Fried Pickle Potato Skins with Bacon and Cheddar 17
Air Fryer Chicken Florentine 18
Air Fryer Duck Confit...18
Arancini (Italian Rice Balls) 18
Fried Chicken and Biscuit Sliders with Honey Butter 19
Air Fryer Chicken and Mushroom Vol-au-Vent 19
Air Fryer Porcini Mushroom Risotto 19
Air Fryer Chicken Piccata 20
Air Fryer Paella 20
Air Fryer Chicken Kiev 21
Air Fryer Veal Piccata...21
Air Fryer Coq au Vin 21
Air Fryer Truffle Risotto 22
Air Fryer Chicken Alfredo 22

Chapter 3 Dinner 23

Fried Cheese-Stuffed Portobello Mushrooms...23
Crispy Fried Okra with Cajun Remoulade 23
Air Fryer Steak Fajitas 23
Air Fryer Duck Breast with Port Wine Reduction 24
Air Fryer Greek Potatoes 24
Air Fryer Beef and Mushroom Duxelles Crepes 24
Air Fryer Mac and Cheese 25
Air Fryer Gourmet Pizza...25
Steak and Kidney Pie 26

Roast Chicken with Vegetables 26
Beef and Ale Stew 26
Spaghetti Bolognese 27
Thai Green Curry 27

Chapter 4 Beef, Pork and Lamb 28

Air Fryer Pork Belly 28
Air Fryer Beef Wellington with Foie Gras 28
Air Fryer Beef Rouladen 28
Air Fryer Stuffed Flank Steak 29
Air Fryer Parmesan-Crusted Rack of Lamb 29
Air Fryer Beef and Black Bean Stir-Fry 29
Air Fryer Pork Belly Bao Buns 30
Air Fryer Beef Stir-Fry 30
Air Fryer Beef Tournedos Rossini 30
Air Fryer Italian Meatballs 31
Air Fryer Beef Tenderloin with Gorgonzola Sauce 31
Air Fryer Beef and Blue Cheese-Stuffed Peppers 31
Air Fryer Beef Wellington 31
Air Fryer Herb-Crusted Lamb Chops 32
Italian Prosciutto-Wrapped Beef Tenderloin 32
Mexican Chorizo Stuffed Jalapeño Poppers 32
Spicy Korean Pork Belly 33
Vietnamese Grilled Lemongrass Pork Chops 33

Chapter 5 Fish and Seafood 34

Air Fryer Asian Glazed Salmon 34
Air Fryer Crab-Stuffed Shrimp 34
Fried Shrimp Po' Boy 34
Parmesan Crusted Fish 35
Air Fryer Cajun Shrimp and Sausage Foil Packets 35
Air Fryer Teriyaki Salmon 35
Air Fryer Cilantro-Lime Shrimp 35
Air Fryer Seafood Medley 36
Air Fryer Crab Cakes 36
Air Fryer Truffle-Crusted Scallops 36
Tempura-Battered Shrimp 36
Air Fryer Salmon with Dill Cream Sauce 37
Air Fryer Lemon Herb Salmon Patties 37

Air Fryer Shrimp Scampi 37
Air Fryer Salmon en Papillote 38
Air Fryer Lobster Tails 38
Middle Eastern Za'atar Crusted Halibut 38
Moroccan Grilled Swordfish with Harissa 39
Cajun Shrimp and Sausage Foil Packets...39
Chimichurri Grilled Shrimp 39
Lobster Mac and Cheese Bites 39
Salmon Croquettes with Lemon-Dill Sauce 40

Chapter 6 Sides and Appetizers 41

Air Fryer Chimichurri Chicken Thighs 41
Air Fryer Crab-Stuffed Mushrooms with Garlic Butter 41
Air Fryer Honey BBQ Chicken Sliders 41
Crispy Fried Asparagus and Prosciutto Bundles 42
Korean BBQ Chicken Wings 42
Air Fryer Lemon Pepper Chicken Wings 42
Crispy Fried Brussels Sprout and Bacon Salad 43
Air Fryer Crab Rangoon Dip 43
Fried Goat Cheese Salad with Candied Pecans and Raspberry Vinaigrette 43
Sweet and Spicy Chicken Wings 44
Crispy Fried Mushrooms 44
Sesame Chicken Wings 44
Air Fryer Orange Chicken 45
Teriyaki Chicken Wings 45
Crispy Fried Tofu Nuggets 45
Coconut Shrimp Salad 46
Air Fryer Crab-Stuffed Mushrooms 46
Fried Green Tomato BLT 46
Air Fryer Spicy Chicken Tenders 47
Korean Fried Chicken (Yangnyeom Chicken) 47
Fried Jalapeno Popper Dip 47
Air Fryer Chicken Liver Pâté 48
Fried Plantains 48
Air Fryer Sesame Ginger Tofu 48
Air Fryer Onion Rings 49
Air Fryer Garlic Parmesan Wings 49
Pakoras (Indian Vegetable Fritters) 49
Stuffed Mushrooms..49

Potato Latkes 50
Cauliflower Buffalo Bites 50
Mini Cornish Pasties 50

Chapter 7 Veggie and Vegetarian 51

Fried Avocado and Black Bean Quesadillas 51
Crispy Fried Brussels Sprout Caesar Salad 51
Fried Avocado Tacos with Cilantro Lime Sauce...51
Crispy Fried Zucchini Blossoms Stuffed with Goat Cheese 52
Buffalo Cauliflower Wraps 52
Crispy Fried Asparagus 53
Crispy Fried Tofu 53
Garlic Herb Roasted Chickpeas 53
Air Fryer Vegetarian Spring Rolls 53
Air Fryer Ratatouille Quiche 54
Fried Mozzarella Caprese Salad 54
Crispy Fried Green Bean and Mushroom Stir-Fry 54
Crispy Fried Avocado and Black Bean Tacos with Lime Crema 55
Crispy Fried Zucchini Noodle Salad with Lemon Vinaigrette 55
Air Fryer Ratatouille 56
Air Fryer Stuffed Acorn Squash with Quinoa and Cranberries 56
Air Fryer Cabbage Steaks 56
Air Fryer Green Bean Fries..57
Green Beans with Garlic 57
Eggplant Fries 57
Roasted Carrot Fries 57
Broiled Asparagus with Lemon and Parmesan 58
Dehydrated Vegetable Chips with Sea Salt...58
Broiled Eggplant with Garlic and Tahini Sauce 58

chapter 8 Snacks 59

Air Fryer BBQ Ribs 59
Air Fryer Honey Mustard Chicken Tenders 59
Fried Chicken and Waffle Skewers with Maple Sriracha Glaze 59
Fried Cheeseburger Egg Rolls 60
Crispy Fried Coconut Tofu with Sweet Chili Sauce 60
Buffalo Chicken Sliders 60
Air Fryer Apple Chips...61
Fried Mozzarella Balls 61

Crispy Fried Onion Strings 61
Egg Rolls..61
Chicken Satay Skewers 62
Air Fryer Kale Chips 62
Air Fryer Mini Tacos 62
Air Fryer Donuts 63
Molten Lava Cakes 63
Air Fryer Churro Bites 63
Mini Fruit Pies 64
Corn Dogs 64
Fried Ravioli 64
Air Fryer Donut Twists 65
S'mores Crescent Rolls 65
Fried Cheese Curds 65
Zeppoles (Italian Fried Dough Balls) 65
Air Fryer Jerk Chicken Wings 66
Ham and Cheese Croissant Bites 66
Mini Apple Hand Pies with Salted Caramel Drizzle 66
Air Fryer S'mores 67
Churros with Chocolate Sauce 67

chapter 9 Dessert 68

Fried Banana Spring Rolls with Nutella Dip 68
Air Fryer Mini Cheesecakes 68
Air Fryer Apple Fritters 68
Funnel Cakes 69
Air Fryer Brownies 69
Air Fryer Cinnamon Rolls 69
Air Fryer Blueberry Muffins 69
Blueberry Lemon Cornmeal Muffins 70
Air Fryer Chocolate-Dipped Coconut Macaroons 70
Air Fryer Chocolate Chip Cookies 70

Introduction

Getting To Know Ninja Dual Zone Air Fryers

Air Fryers are popular countertop appliances that are proving to be indispensable in the kitchen. The Ninja line of Dual Zone Air Fryers are innovative kitchen appliances that have gained popularity for their ability to provide a healthier alternative to traditional frying methods. These air fryers are designed to deliver crispy and delicious results by utilizing hot air circulation instead of oil. With their dual-zone cooking capabilities and versatile functions, they offer a convenient and efficient way to prepare a wide range of meals.

The dual-zone cooking feature is one of the standout aspects of Ninja Dual Zone Air Fryers. It allows you to cook two separate dishes simultaneously, thanks to the independent cooking zones. Each zone has its own temperature and cooking time settings, enabling you to prepare different foods with different requirements all at once. This feature is especially beneficial when you need to cook multiple items for a meal or when you want to prepare a variety of appetizers or snacks.

These air fryers offer precise temperature control, typically ranging from 105°F to 450°F (40°C to 232°C). With the digital control panel, you can easily set and adjust the cooking time and temperature according to your preferences. This level of precision control ensures that your food is cooked to perfection, whether you're air frying, roasting, broiling, dehydrating, or reheating.

Ninja Dual Zone Air Fryers come with pre-programmed cooking presets that simplify the cooking process. These presets are designed to provide optimal cooking settings for specific types of food, such as fries, chicken wings, fish, vegetables, and more. By selecting the appropriate preset, you can achieve consistent and delicious results without the need for manual temperature and time adjustments. The presets take the guesswork out of cooking, making it easier for both beginners and experienced cooks to achieve satisfying meals.

To facilitate even cooking, Ninja Dual Zone Air Fryers are equipped with powerful fans and advanced airflow technology. This ensures that the hot air is evenly distributed throughout the cooking chamber, eliminating any hot or cold spots. As a result, your food is cooked consistently and uniformly, without the need for flipping or rotating during the cooking process.

Why Choose The Ninja Dual Zone (Benefits)

The reasons behind choosing to use Ninja Dual Zone Air Fryers may differ from one individual to the other. These innovative kitchen appliances provide a range of benefits that make them the indispensable tools they are. You can find some of these reasons below:

- **Healthier Cooking:** One of the primary advantages of Ninja Dual Zone Air Fryers is their ability to provide a healthier alternative to traditional frying methods. These air fryers use hot air circulation to cook food, requiring little to no oil. By significantly reducing oil usage, they help to decrease calorie intake and reduce the consumption of unhealthy fats, making your meals healthier overall.
- **Reduced Fat Content:** With Ninja Dual Zone Air Fryers, you can achieve crispy and delicious results without the need for excessive oil. The hot air circulation technology ensures that the food is evenly cooked and achieves a crispy texture, similar to deep frying, but with significantly less oil. This reduction in fat content can promote heart health and contribute to a balanced diet.
- **Versatile Cooking Options:** Ninja Dual Zone Air Fryers offer versatility in cooking. In addition to air frying, they often come with multiple cooking functions such as roasting, broiling, dehydrating, and reheating. This versatility allows you to experiment with various recipes and expand your culinary options, making it a versatile appliance for different cooking needs. Whether you want to roast vegetables, broil chicken, dehydrate fruits,

or reheat leftovers, the variety of cooking options offered by these air fryers provides flexibility and convenience. You can easily switch between different cooking modes to suit your preferences and create different meals with ease.

- Time Efficiency: These air fryers are known for their ability to cook food quickly, saving you time in the kitchen. The hot air circulation technology facilitates fast and efficient cooking, reducing the cooking time compared to conventional methods. Additionally, the dual-zone cooking feature allows you to cook multiple dishes simultaneously, further optimizing your cooking time.
- Energy Efficiency - Ninja Dual Zone Air Fryers are energy-efficient appliances that help you save energy and reduce your carbon footprint. These air fryers utilize hot air circulation technology to cook food, requiring less energy compared to traditional cooking methods such as deep frying or oven baking. The efficient distribution of hot air within the cooking chamber ensures that the food is cooked evenly and quickly, further contributing to energy savings. By using less energy during cooking, Ninja Dual Zone Air Fryers help you save on your electricity bills while minimizing environmental impact.
- Consistent Cooking Results: Ninja Dual Zone Air Fryers are designed to provide consistent cooking results. The advanced airflow technology and powerful fans ensure that the hot air is evenly distributed throughout the cooking chamber, resulting in uniform cooking. This eliminates the need for flipping or rotating the food during the cooking process, saving you effort and ensuring consistent results every time.
- Easy to Use: These air fryers are generally user-friendly, featuring intuitive controls and digital displays. The pre-programmed cooking presets simplify the cooking process by offering optimal settings for various types of food. This makes it easy for both beginners and experienced cooks to achieve delicious and well-cooked meals with minimal effort.
- Easy to Clean: Cleaning up after cooking can be a hassle, but Ninja Dual Zone Air Fryers are designed with convenience in mind. These air fryers typically feature non-stick cooking baskets and trays, which make them easy to clean. The non-stick coating prevents food from sticking to the surfaces, reducing the effort required for cleaning. Many components are also dishwasher-safe, allowing you to simply place them in the dishwasher for hassle-free cleaning. The easy-to-clean design of these air fryers saves you time and effort, making them a convenient addition to your kitchen.
- Spacious Cooking Capacity: Ninja Dual Zone Air Fryers typically feature a spacious cooking basket that can accommodate a large quantity of food. This makes them ideal for families or for cooking meals for gatherings and parties. The large cooking capacity allows you to prepare meals in larger portions, saving you time and effort in multiple cooking batches.
- Recipe Inspiration: Ninja often provides recipe books or digital resources to inspire users like you and help you explore various cooking possibilities. These recipes can guide you in creating a wide range of dishes, from appetizers and main courses to desserts, allowing you to make the most of your air fryer.
- Brand Reputation: Ninja is a well-known brand in the kitchen appliance industry, known for its quality and performance. Investing in a Ninja Dual Zone Air Fryer means you can rely on a reputable brand, backed by a strong customer support system and warranties.

Tips and Tricks For Using The Ninja Dual Zone Air Fryer

Getting a new Nnja Dual Zone Air fryer can be an exciting experience and understanding some quick tips and tricks can help you get acquainted with this functional air fryer easily. Some tips for the Ninja Dual Zone Air Fryer are:

Read the Manual: Before using your Ninja Dual Zone Air Fryer, thoroughly read the instruction manual provided by the manufacturer. This will familiarize you with the appliance's features, functions, and safety guidelines.

- Preheat the Air Fryer: It's generally recommended to preheat the air fryer before cooking. This ensures that the cooking chamber reaches the

desired temperature and helps achieve optimal cooking results. Follow the manufacturer's instructions for preheating time and temperature.
- Use the Dual Zone Feature: Take advantage of the dual-zone cooking feature of the Ninja Dual Zone Air Fryer. This feature allows you to cook different foods simultaneously at different temperatures and cooking times, maximizing efficiency and convenience. Utilize the separate cooking zones to cook a main dish and side dish or to prepare multiple batches of the same food.
- Use the Smart Finish feature: When using both zones for cooking, it can be a bit annoying when one dish gets prepared before the other and you have to wait. Now, with the Smart Finish feature, all you need to do is press the "Smart Finish" button and the air fryer finishes cooking both baskets at the same time. This is regardless of the difference in cooking times or cooking temperatures of both dishes. Both zones get the food properly prepared at the same time.
- Adjust Cooking Times and Temperatures: Cooking times and temperatures may vary depending on the recipe and the quantity of food being cooked. Experiment with adjusting the cooking times and temperatures to achieve your desired level of crispiness and doneness. Keep track of your adjustments for future reference.
- Flip and Shake: To ensure even cooking, flip or shake the food halfway through the cooking process. This helps to distribute heat evenly and achieve consistent results. Use tongs or a spatula to flip larger items, and gently shake the basket to toss smaller ingredients.
- Avoid Overcrowding: Avoid overcrowding the cooking basket, as it can hinder proper air circulation and result in uneven cooking. If you have a large quantity of food to cook, consider cooking it in batches to maintain optimal air circulation and achieve crispier results.
- Preparing Food: When preparing food for air frying, pat dry any excess moisture from the ingredients. This helps to achieve crispier textures. If desired, you can lightly coat the food with a small amount of oil or use a cooking spray to enhance browning and prevent sticking.
- Seasoning and Flavoring: Experiment with different seasonings and flavorings to enhance the taste of your air-fried dishes. Sprinkle herbs, spices, or marinades onto the food before cooking to infuse flavor. You can also brush sauces or glazes onto the food during the cooking process for added taste.
- Cleaning and Maintenance: After each use, allow the air fryer to cool down before cleaning. Remove the cooking basket and any removable parts and wash them with warm soapy water or place them in the dishwasher if they are dishwasher-safe. Wipe the interior and exterior surfaces of the air fryer with a damp cloth. Regularly clean the air intake and exhaust vents to ensure optimal performance.
- Explore Recipes and Resources: To make the most of your Ninja Dual Zone Air Fryer, explore various recipe books, online resources, and cooking communities for inspiration and guidance. There are numerous recipes available specifically tailored for air fryers, providing ideas for appetizers, main courses, sides, and even desserts.

Cleaning And Maintenance

The build of the Ninja Dual Zone Air Fryer makes it an easy to clean appliance and maintain. To ensure your Ninja Dual Zone Air Fryer stays at optimal condition, it is important to imbibe proper cleaning and maintenance practices that are specific to the unique brand. Find some of the cleaning and maintenance tips below:
- Unplug the Air Fryer: Before cleaning, ensure that the air fryer is unplugged and has completely cooled down to a safe temperature.
- Remove Removable Parts: Take out the cooking basket, crisper plate or tray, and any other removable parts from the air fryer.
- Hand Wash or Dishwasher: Check the manufacturer's instructions to determine if the removable parts are dishwasher-safe. If they are, place them in the dishwasher for cleaning. Otherwise, wash them with warm soapy water using a non-abrasive sponge or cloth.
- Regular Cleaning: Clean your Ninja Dual Zone Air Fryer after each use to prevent the buildup of grease, food particles, and odors. Regular cleaning helps maintain the performance and longevity of the appliance.

- Soak Stubborn Stains: If there are stubborn food stains or residue on the removable parts, you can soak them in warm soapy water for a few minutes to loosen the debris before washing.
- Wipe the Interior and Exterior: Use a damp cloth or sponge to wipe the interior and exterior surfaces of the air fryer. Avoid using abrasive cleaners or scouring pads that may damage the finish.
- Clean the Heating Element: Gently wipe the heating element with a damp cloth or sponge. Be cautious not to apply excessive pressure or use abrasive materials that may damage the heating element.
- Clean the Air Intake and Exhaust Vents: Regularly clean the air intake and exhaust vents to remove any dust or debris that may affect the air circulation. You can use a soft brush or a vacuum cleaner with a brush attachment to clean these areas.
- Handle the Power Cord with Care: Avoid pulling or twisting the power cord forcefully, as this can damage the cord or the electrical connections. Handle the power cord carefully and ensure it is not tangled or pinched.
- Store Properly: When not in use, store the Ninja Dual Zone Air Fryer in a clean and dry location. Make sure the cord is neatly wrapped and secured to prevent any accidental damage.
- Dry Thoroughly: Ensure that all the parts are completely dry before reassembling and storing the air fryer. Moisture can lead to odors or even mold growth if not properly dried.
- Avoid Abrasive Cleaners: Use only mild dish soap and non-abrasive sponges or cloths when cleaning the air fryer. Avoid using harsh or abrasive cleaners that may scratch or damage the surfaces.
- Avoid Submerging the Air Fryer: Do not submerge the main unit or the control panel in water or any other liquid. This can cause electrical damage and compromise the safety of the appliance.
- Refer to the Manual: Always refer to the instruction manual provided by the manufacturer for specific cleaning and maintenance guidelines. The manual may include additional tips or precautions specific to your model.

About The Recipes

The Air Fryer being the useful tool that it is, has taken the kitchen by storm. Recognozing this detail, the goal of this cookbook is to take advantage of the Air Fryer and expose users to the limitless possibilities with the Air fryer. Whether you're a seasoned chef or a novice, this book is a perfect guide.

In this ebook, i have put together 180 recipes that range from easy to prepare recipes to the ones with a little challenge. These recipes help fully understand the intricacies of the working of you air fryer as well as helping you items simultaneously at different temperatures and times. This is particularly valuable when preparing a complete meal with various components, such as chicken, vegetables, and dessert. This also means that you don't have to wait till any dish gets ready first to continue it

With the air fryer, you can achieve specific textures and flavors in your dishes. It's an excellent tool for testing and perfecting your cooking techniques. With the air fryer, you can achieve specific textures and flavors in your dishes. It's an excellent tool for testing and perfecting your cooking techniques.n.. With the air fryer, you can achieve specific textures and flavors in your dishes. It's an excellent tool for testing and perfecting your cooking techniques.

The presets are programmed to deliver consistent results for specific types of food. This ensures that your dishes turn out well-cooked and delicious every time, reducing the risk of overcooking or undercooking. While presets are a great starting point, they are not one-size-fits-all. You can often adjust the temperature and cooking time to customize the presets to your preferences. This flexibility allows you to fine-tune the cooking process for specific recipes.

You can also adapt traditional recipes to the air fryer, which can lead to creative variations and unique flavors. This encourages culinary creativity and experimentation.

There are breakfast, salads, snacks and even dessert recipes for you to experiment with using the air fryer. The recipes are suitable for parties, family dinners or just to satisfy your curious cooking skill. Keep reading to find out.

chapter 1 Breakfast

Fried Green Tomato and Pimento Cheese Grilled Cheese

Serves 2 / Prep Time: 15 minutes / Cook Time: 15 minutes

- For the Fried Green Tomatoes:
- 2 medium green tomatoes (about 300g)
- 1/2 cup all-purpose flour (60g)
- 2 large eggs, beaten
- 1 cup panko breadcrumbs (120g)
- Salt and black pepper to taste
- Vegetable oil for frying
- For the Pimento Cheese:
- 1/2 cup grated sharp cheddar cheese (60g)
- 1/4 cup mayonnaise (60g)
- 2 tablespoons diced pimentos
- 1/4 teaspoon garlic powder
- Salt and black pepper to taste
- For the Grilled Cheese:
- 4 slices of bread
- 2 tablespoons butter (30g)

1. Start by preparing the Fried Green Tomatoes. Slice the green tomatoes into 1/4-inch thick rounds.
2. In one bowl, place all-purpose flour. In another bowl, add the beaten eggs. In a third bowl, fill it with panko breadcrumbs, salt, and black pepper.
3. In a separate bowl, mix grated cheddar cheese, mayonnaise, diced pimentos, garlic powder, salt, and black pepper to create the pimento cheese spread.
4. Preheat your deep fryer or a large, deep skillet with vegetable oil to 350°F (175°C).
5. Dip each green tomato round into the flour, then the beaten eggs, and finally coat it with the breadcrumb mixture.
6. Carefully place the coated green tomato rounds into the hot oil and fry for about 2-3 minutes or until they are golden brown and crispy. Remove with a slotted spoon and place on paper towels to drain excess oil.
7. Spread a generous amount of pimento cheese on one side of each slice of bread.
8. Place the Fried Green Tomatoes between two slices of bread, cheese side in, to make a sandwich.
9. Heat a skillet over medium heat, melt the butter, and grill the sandwiches until the bread is golden brown and the cheese is melted.
10. Slice the sandwiches in half and serve.

Air Fryer Pigs in a Blanket

Serves 2 / Prep Time: 10 minutes / Cook Time: 8 minutes

- 4 mini cocktail sausages (150g)
- 4 crescent roll dough triangles
- Mustard or ketchup for dipping

1. Preheat your air fryer to 375°F (190°C).
2. While the air fryer is preheating, wrap each cocktail sausage in a crescent roll dough triangle. Start at the wider end and roll it up, sealing the edges.
3. Place the wrapped sausages in the preheated air fryer basket.
4. Cook the pigs in a blanket at 375°F (190°C) for about 8 minutes or until they are golden brown and the dough is cooked through.
5. Remove from the air fryer and let them cool for a minute.

Fried Zucchini Sticks

Serves 2 / Prep Time: 15 minutes / Cook Time: 10 minutes

- 2 medium zucchinis (400g)
- 100g all-purpose flour
- 2 eggs, beaten
- 150g breadcrumbs
- 1 teaspoon dried oregano
- Salt and pepper to taste
- Vegetable oil for frying

1. Start by trimming the ends of the zucchinis and cutting them into sticks.
2. In three separate bowls, place the all-purpose flour in one, the beaten eggs in another, and mix the breadcrumbs with dried oregano, salt, and pepper in the third.
3. Dip each zucchini stick into the flour, then the beaten eggs, and finally coat them in the breadcrumb mixture. Place them on a plate.
4. Preheat your deep fryer or a large, deep skillet with vegetable oil to 350°F (175°C).
5. Carefully place the breaded zucchini sticks into the hot oil and fry for about 2-3 minutes or until they are golden brown and crispy. Remove with a slotted spoon and place on paper towels to drain excess oil.

Air Fryer Veggie Burger

Serves 2 / Prep Time: 10 minutes / Cook Time: 15 minutes

- 2 veggie burger patties (200g each)
- 4 whole wheat burger buns
- 1 tomato, sliced
- 1/2 red onion, thinly sliced
- Lettuce leaves
- Ketchup, mustard, or your favorite condiments

1. Preheat your Ninja Foodi Dual Zone Air Fryer to 375°F (190°C).
2. Place the veggie burger patties in the air fryer basket.
3. Cook the veggie burgers at 375°F (190°C) for about 12-15 minutes, flipping halfway through, until they are heated through and have a crispy exterior.
4. While the burgers are cooking, split and lightly toast the whole wheat burger buns.
5. Place a lettuce leaf on the bottom half of each toasted bun.
6. Add a veggie burger patty on top of the lettuce.
7. Add a slice of tomato and some red onion slices.
8. Spread your choice of condiments (ketchup, mustard, etc.) on the top half of the bun.
9. Assemble the burger by placing the top half on the burger patty.
10. Serve the veggie burger with your favorite side dishes.

Buffalo Cauliflower Pizza Bites

Serves 2 / Prep Time: 20 minutes / Cook Time: 15 minutes

- For the Buffalo Cauliflower:
- 300g cauliflower florets
- 30g all-purpose flour
- 5g garlic powder
- 5g onion powder
- 5g salt
- 5g black pepper
- 1 egg
- 30g hot sauce
- For the Pizza Bites:
- 4 small whole wheat pita bread rounds
- 60g marinara sauce
- 60g shredded mozzarella cheese
- 5g dried oregano

1. In a bowl, combine the flour, garlic powder, onion powder, salt, and black pepper.
2. In another bowl, whisk together the egg and hot sauce.
3. Dip the cauliflower florets into the flour mixture, then into the egg and hot sauce mixture, and back into the flour mixture, ensuring they are well-coated.
4. Preheat your Ninja Foodi Dual Zone Air Fryer to 375°F (190°C) using the "Air Fry" setting.
5. Place the cauliflower in the air fryer basket and air fry for about 12-15 minutes or until they are crispy and golden.
6. While the cauliflower is cooking, prepare the pizza bites. Spread marinara sauce over each pita bread, sprinkle with mozzarella cheese, and a pinch of dried oregano.
7. Once the cauliflower is done, arrange them on the pita bread rounds.
8. Place the pizza bites in the air fryer and air fry for an additional 3-4 minutes or until the cheese is melted and bubbly.

Chicken and Waffles

Serves 2 / Prep Time: 20 minutes / Cook Time: 20 minutes

- For the Fried Chicken:
- 300g boneless, skinless chicken breasts, cut into strips
- 100g all-purpose flour
- 5g paprika
- 5g garlic powder
- 5g salt
- 5g black pepper
- 1 egg
- Cooking oil, for frying
- For the Waffles:
- 150g all-purpose flour
- 5g baking powder
- 5g sugar
- 2g salt
- 1 egg
- 240ml milk
- 30ml melted butter

1. In a bowl, combine the all-purpose flour, paprika, garlic powder, salt, and black pepper for the chicken coating.
2. In another bowl, beat the egg. Dip each chicken strip into the egg, then into the flour mixture, ensuring they are well-coated.
3. Preheat your Ninja Foodi Dual Zone Air Fryer to 375°F (190°C) using the "Air Fry" setting.
4. Lightly grease the air fryer basket with cooking oil.
5. Place the coated chicken strips in the air fryer basket.
6. Air fry for about 10-12 minutes, flipping the chicken strips halfway through, until they are crispy and cooked through.
7. While the chicken is cooking, prepare the waffle

batter. In a separate bowl, mix the all-purpose flour, baking powder, sugar, and salt. In another bowl, beat the egg, and then add the milk and melted butter.
8. Combine the wet and dry ingredients, and mix until just combined. Preheat your waffle iron and cook waffles according to its instructions.
9. Serve the crispy fried chicken strips with the waffles and your favorite toppings such as maple syrup or hot sauce.

Air Fryer Beef Taquitos

Serves 2 / Prep Time: 15 minutes / Cook Time: 15 minutes

- For the Beef Filling:
- 200g ground beef
- 5g chili powder
- 5g cumin
- 5g garlic powder
- 5g onion powder
- 5g salt
- 5g black pepper
- 60g shredded cheddar cheese
- For the Taquito Assembly:
- 4 small flour tortillas
- Cooking oil, for brushing

1. In a skillet, cook the ground beef over medium-high heat, breaking it apart as it cooks.
2. Once the beef is browned, add chili powder, cumin, garlic powder, onion powder, salt, and black pepper. Stir well and cook for a few minutes. Remove from heat and let it cool slightly.
3. Preheat your Ninja Foodi Dual Zone Air Fryer to 375°F (190°C) using the "Air Fry" setting.
4. Place a portion of the beef filling and some shredded cheddar cheese on each tortilla. Roll up each tortilla tightly into a taquito.
5. Brush the taquitos lightly with cooking oil.
6. Place the taquitos in the air fryer basket.
7. Air fry for about 10-12 minutes, or until the taquitos are crispy and golden brown.

Air Fryer Empanadas

Serves 2 / Prep Time: 25 minutes / Cook Time: 12 minutes

- 150g ground beef
- 150g diced onion
- 100g diced bell pepper
- 75g diced green olives
- 5g minced garlic
- 5g ground cumin
- 5g paprika
- Salt and black pepper to taste
- 200g empanada dough (store-bought or homemade)

1. In a skillet, heat some oil over medium heat. Add the diced onion and bell pepper, and sauté until they are softened.
2. Add the ground beef, minced garlic, ground cumin, paprika, salt, and black pepper. Cook until the beef is browned and cooked through. Stir in the diced green olives and remove from heat.
3. Preheat your air fryer to 375°F (190°C) using the "Air Fry" setting.
4. Roll out the empanada dough and cut it into 4 equal rounds.
5. Place a spoonful of the beef filling onto one half of each dough round. Fold the other half over to create a semi-circle and crimp the edges to seal.
6. Lightly grease the air fryer basket and place the empanadas inside.
7. Air fry for about 10-12 minutes or until they are golden brown and crispy.

Coconut Shrimp Tacos

Serves 2 / Prep Time: 25 minutes / Cook Time: 12 minutes

- 200g large shrimp, peeled and deveined
- 50g shredded coconut
- 50g breadcrumbs
- 2g salt
- 2g black pepper
- 1 egg
- Cooking oil, for spraying
- 4 small flour tortillas
- 100g shredded lettuce
- 50g diced tomatoes
- 50g diced red onion
- 50g diced pineapple
- 30g chopped cilantro
- Lime wedges

1. In one bowl, combine shredded coconut and breadcrumbs. In another bowl, beat the egg.
2. Season the shrimp with salt and black pepper.
3. Dredge each shrimp in the breadcrumb and coconut mixture, then dip it in the beaten egg, and coat it again with the breadcrumb mixture.
4. Preheat your Ninja Foodi Dual Zone Air Fryer to 375°F (190°C) using the "Air Fry" setting.
5. Lightly grease the air fryer basket with cooking oil and place the coconut shrimp inside.
6. Air fry for about 10-12 minutes, turning them over halfway through, until they are golden and crispy.
7. While the shrimp is cooking, assemble the tacos by placing lettuce, tomatoes, red onion, pineapple,

and cilantro on each tortilla.
8. Once the shrimp is done, place a few pieces on each taco. Serve with lime wedges.

Air Fryer Chicken Quesadillas

Serves 2 / Prep Time: 15 minutes / Cook Time: 10 minutes

- For the Quesadillas:
- 2 large flour tortillas
- 200g cooked chicken, shredded
- 100g shredded cheddar cheese
- 50g diced bell peppers
- 50g diced onions
- 10g taco seasoning
- Cooking spray

1. In a bowl, mix the cooked shredded chicken and taco seasoning until well coated.
2. Place one tortilla on a clean surface.
3. Layer half of the shredded cheese, chicken, diced bell peppers, diced onions, and the remaining cheese.
4. Top with the second tortilla.
5. Preheat your Ninja Foodi Dual Zone Air Fryer to 375°F (190°C).
6. Spray the air fryer basket with cooking spray.
7. Carefully place the quesadilla in the air fryer basket.
8. Air fry at 375°F (190°C) for 5 minutes, flip the quesadilla, and air fry for an additional 5 minutes or until it's golden and crispy.
9. Remove, let it cool for a minute, then slice and serve.

Air Fryer Taquitos

Serves 2 / Prep Time: 20 minutes / Cook Time: 15 minutes

- 150g cooked and shredded chicken
- 100g shredded cheddar cheese
- 50g cream cheese, softened
- 50g diced green chilies
- 1/2 tsp ground cumin
- 1/2 tsp chili powder
- 1/4 tsp garlic powder
- 1/4 tsp onion powder
- Salt and pepper to taste
- 6 small flour tortillas
- Cooking spray

1. In a mixing bowl, combine the shredded chicken, cheddar cheese, cream cheese, diced green chilies, cumin, chili powder, garlic powder, onion powder, salt, and pepper. Mix until well combined.
2. Lay out a tortilla, and place a portion of the mixture in the center.
3. Roll up the tortilla tightly, securing the filling inside. Place it seam-side down on a plate. Repeat with the remaining tortillas.
4. Preheat your Ninja Foodi Dual Zone Air Fryer to 360°F (180°C).
5. Spray the taquitos lightly with cooking spray to help them turn golden and crispy.
6. Place the taquitos in the air fryer basket, ensuring they are not touching.
7. Set the air fryer to 360°F (180°C) and air fry for 12-15 minutes or until they are golden brown and crispy.

Air Fryer Gourmet Grilled Cheese

Serves 2 / Prep Time: 10 minutes / Cook Time: 10 minutes

- For the Grilled Cheese:
- 4 slices of bread (about 100g)
- 30g unsalted butter, softened
- 100g sharp cheddar cheese, shredded
- 100g Swiss cheese, shredded
- 50g prosciutto or bacon (optional)
- 50g arugula or baby spinach (optional)
- For Dipping:
- 30g tomato soup

1. Preheat your Ninja Foodi Dual Zone Air Fryer to 375°F (190°C) on the "Air Fry" setting.
2. Butter one side of each slice of bread.
3. On the non-buttered side, layer the cheddar and Swiss cheese. Add prosciutto or bacon and arugula or baby spinach if desired.
4. Place another slice of bread on top with the buttered side facing out.
5. In one air fryer zone, place the prepared grilled cheese sandwiches.
6. Air fry at 375°F (190°C) for about 5-7 minutes, flip them, and air fry for an additional 5-7 minutes until they are golden brown and the cheese is melted
7. In the other air fryer zone, place a small rmekin of tomato soup.
8. Serve your Gourmet Grilled Cheese with a side of tomato soup for dipping.
9. Enjoy your Air Fryer Gourmet Grilled Cheese!

Crispy Fried Sweet Potato Hash Browns

Serves 2 / Prep Time: 15 minutes / Cook Time: 15 minutes

- 2 medium sweet potatoes, peeled and grated (about 200g each)
- 5g salt
- 5g black pepper
- 5g garlic powder

- 5g onion powder
- 10g cornstarch
- 20g olive oil

1. Preheat your Ninja Foodi Dual Zone Air Fryer to 375°F (190°C) on the "Air Fry" setting.
2. Place the grated sweet potatoes in a clean kitchen towel, gather the ends, and squeeze out any excess moisture.
3. In a bowl, season the grated sweet potatoes with salt, black pepper, garlic powder, onion powder, and cornstarch. Toss to coat.
4. In one air fryer zone, arrange the seasoned sweet potatoes in a single layer.
5. Air fry at 375°F (190°C) for about 12-15 minutes, turning them once or twice during cooking, until they are crispy and cooked through.
6. Drizzle with olive oil and air fry for an additional 2-3 minutes until they are extra crispy.
7. Serve your Crispy Fried Sweet Potato Hash Browns.
8. Enjoy these delicious, crunchy hash browns as a side dish or breakfast!

Air Fryer Egg and Veggie Breakfast Pockets

Serves 2 / Prep Time: 15 minutes / Cook Time: 10 minutes

- 2 sheets puff pastry (100g each)
- 4 large eggs
- 100g bell peppers, diced
- 50g onion, diced
- 50g shredded cheese
- Salt and black pepper to taste

1. Preheat your Ninja Foodi Dual Zone Air Fryer to 375°F (190°C) on the "Air Fry" setting.
2. In a bowl, beat the eggs and mix in the diced bell peppers, diced onion, shredded cheese, salt, and black pepper.
3. Place one sheet of puff pastry in each zone.
4. Spoon the egg and veggie mixture onto one half of each puff pastry sheet.
5. Fold the other half of the puff pastry over the egg mixture and press the edges to seal, creating pockets.
6. Air fry at 375°F (190°C) for about 10 minutes, or until the pastry is golden brown and the eggs are cooked.
7. Serve your Egg and Veggie Breakfast Pockets hot.
8. Enjoy your breakfast!

Air-Fried Bacon-Wrapped Egg Cups

Serves 2 / Prep Time: 15 minutes / Cook Time: 10 minutes

- 4 slices bacon
- 4 large eggs
- Salt and black pepper to taste
- Fresh chives, chopped (for garnish)

1. Preheat your Ninja Foodi Dual Zone Air Fryer to 375°F (190°C) on the "Air Fry" setting.
2. Wrap each slice of bacon around the inside of a muffin cup in a muffin tin to create a cup for the egg.
3. Carefully crack an egg into each bacon-wrapped cup.
4. Air fry at 375°F (190°C) for about 10 minutes, or until the bacon is crispy and the egg is cooked to your desired level.
5. Sprinkle with salt, black pepper, and chopped fresh chives.
6. Serve your Bacon-Wrapped Egg Cups hot.
7. Enjoy your delicious and protein-packed breakfast!

Air Fryer Chili Cheese Dogs

Serves 2 / Prep Time: 10 minutes / Cook Time: 10 minutes

- 2 hot dog buns
- 2 beef or veggie hot dogs
- 100g canned chili
- 60g shredded cheddar cheese

1. Preheat your Ninja Foodi Dual Zone Air Fryer to 350°F (180°C) on the "Air Fry" setting.
2. Warm the canned chili in a microwave-safe container or on the stovetop.
3. Place the hot dog buns in the air fryer basket, cut side down, for about 2 minutes to toast.
4. Place the hot dogs in the air fryer basket and air fry at 350°F (180°C) for about 5 minutes or until heated through and slightly crispy.
5. Once the hot dogs are ready, place them in the toasted buns.
6. Top each hot dog with a generous portion of chili and shredded cheddar cheese.
7. Return the hot dogs to the air fryer and air fry for an additional 2-3 minutes or until the cheese is melted and bubbly.
8. Serve your chili cheese dogs hot and enjoy.

Scotch woodcock (anchovy on toast)

Serves: 2 / Prep Time: 5 minutes / Cook Time: 5 minutes

- 4 slices of bread
- 2 tablespoons of butter
- 4-6 anchovy fillets
- 2 eggs
- Salt and freshly ground black pepper
- Chopped parsley, to serve

1. Preheat the Ninja Dual Zone to Air Fry at 190°C (190°C).
2. Lightly toast the bread slices and spread each slice with butter.
3. Arrange the anchovy fillets on the buttered toast.
4. Crack the eggs into a bowl and whisk together with a fork. Add salt and pepper to taste.
5. Melt the remaining butter in a frying pan over medium heat. Add the eggs to the pan and cook, stirring gently, until they are scrambled and just set.
6. Transfer the scrambled eggs to the Ninja Dual basket and cook for 1-2 minutes until hot.
7. Serve the scrambled eggs on top of the anchovy toast and sprinkle with chopped parsley.

Porridge

Serves: 4 / Prep Time: 20- 25 minutes / Cook Time: 25 minutes or more

- 128g of steel-cut oats
- 750 ml of water
- 1/4 teaspoon salt
- 125 ml of milk (or non-dairy milk)
- Toppings of your choice (e. g. fresh or dried fruit, nuts, seeds, honey, maple syrup)

1. Rinse the steel-cut oats and place them in the Ninja Dual Zone's inner pot with water and salt.
2. Select the "Pressure Cook" function and set the timer for 10 minutes.
3. Once the timer goes off, allow the pressure to release naturally for about 10 minutes before carefully opening the lid.
4. Stir in the milk (or non-dairy milk) and mix well.
5. Serve hot in bowls and top with your desired toppings.

Full English Breakfast

Serves: 4 / Prep time: 10 minutes / Cook Time: 20 -25 minutes

- 4 sausages
- 4 slices of bacon
- 4 eggs
- 1 large tomato, sliced in half
- 4 mushrooms, sliced
- 1 can of baked beans
- Salt and pepper, to taste
- Olive oil or cooking spray

1. Preheat the Ninja Dual Zone air fryer to 190°C using the Air Fry mode.
2. Place the sausages in the air fryer basket and cook for 10 minutes, flipping halfway through.
3. Add the bacon to the air fryer basket and cook for an additional 5-7 minutes, or until crispy.
4. Remove the sausages and bacon from the air fryer and set aside on a plate.
5. Spray the air fryer basket with cooking spray or drizzle with a bit of olive oil.
6. Place the halved tomato, sliced mushrooms, and a pinch of salt and pepper in the air fryer basket.
7. Air fry the vegetables for 5-7 minutes, or until tender and slightly browned.
8. While the vegetables are cooking, heat the baked beans in a small saucepan on the stovetop.
9. Once the vegetables are done, remove them from the air fryer and set aside.
10. Crack the eggs into the air fryer basket and sprinkle with salt and pepper.
11. Air fry the eggs for 3-5 minutes, or until cooked to your liking.
12. To serve, place the sausages, bacon, eggs, tomato, mushrooms, and baked beans on a plate. Season with salt and pepper to taste.

Traditional English Breakfast

Prep time: 10 minutes / Cook time: 16 minutes / Serves 5

- 250g brown mushrooms, cut into quarters
- 2 small tomatoes, halved
- Sea salt and ground black pepper, to taste
- 1/2 tsp red pepper flakes, crushed
- 5 rashers smoked bacon
- 4 links breakfast sausage
- 100g canned baked beans, drained

1. Toss the mushrooms and tomatoes with salt, black pepper, and red pepper. Insert a crisper plate in both drawers. Spray the plates with nonstick cooking oil.
2. Next, add the mushrooms, tomatoes, and bacon to the zone 1 drawer. Add breakfast sausage to the zone 2 drawer.
3. Select zone 1 and pair it with at 180°C for 9 minutes. Select zone 2 and pair it with "AIR FRY" at 200°C for 16 minutes
4. Select "SYNC" followed by the "START/STOP" button. At the halfway point, shake your food or toss it with silicone-tipped tongs to promote even cooking.
5. Place all ingredients on serving plates and serve with canned beans. You can also add black pudding and fried eggs for a complete English breakfast.
6. Bon appétit!

Italian-Style Frittata

Prep time: 10 minutes / Cook time: 14 minutes / Serves 5

- 8 whole eggs
- 150g double cream
- 1 garlic clove, pressed
- 1 medium scallion stalk, thinly sliced
- 50g bacon bits
- 150g cherry tomatoes, halved
- 1 tbsp Italian herb mix
- 1 tsp red pepper flakes
- Sea salt and ground black pepper, to taste

1. Remove a crisper plate from your Ninja Foodi. Line the base of the drawers with baking paper.
2. Preheat the Ninja Foodi to 180°C for 5 minutes.
3. In a bowl, whisk the eggs until frothy; fold in the double cream and mix to combine. Add the other ingredients and whisk until everything is well incorporated.
4. Spoon the frittata mixture into the prepared drawers.
5. Select zone 1 and pair it with "BAKE" at 180°C for 14 minutes. Select "MATCH" followed by the "START/STOP" button.
6. Cut warm frittata into 5 wedges and serve immediately. Bon appétit!

Air Fryer Breakfast Quesadillas

Servings: 2 / Prep Time: 4 mins / Cook Time: 8 mins

- Tortillas
- 2 Eggs
- 50g Cheese
- Sour Cream, Guacamole etc
- Preparation Procedures:

1. Preheat your Ninja Dual Zone Air Fryer at 175 degrees Celsius. That is the perfect temperature for cooking quesadillas.
2. Take out your fry pan and scramble-fry your eggs for the filling. Set this aside when you're done.
3. Take out the tortillas and place them on a clean and flat surface.
4. Prepare your fillings, i. e. the scrambled eggs, and cheese. Spread the scrambled eggs on one half of the tortilla flat.
5. Sprinkle the other half with cheese and fold the tortilla in half.
6. Prepare your Ninja Dual Zone Air Fryer drawers by spraying the non-stick plates with cooking spray or using parchment paper. This will prevent the tortillas from sticking and would aid easy cleaning too.
7. Arrange the quesadillas with enough space in between them on the non-stick plates. The space in between is to ensure the quesadillas cook evenly.
8. Place a heavy oven resistant object or even stick toothpicks down the quesadillas to keep the tortillas closed.
9. Select the "AIR FRY" option and airfry the quesadillas for about 8 minutes. The quesadillas are ready when the tortillas become golden brown and the cheese is melted.
10. Take the quesadillas out and serve with sour cream, guacamole, or any of your favorite cream toppings.

Air Fryer Mini Quiches

Servings: 2 / Prep Time: 5 mins / Cook Time: 12 mins

- 3 large eggs
- 39. 5g milk
- 18. 6g shredded cheese (such as cheddar or Gruyere)
- 35g diced cooked bacon or ham
- 35g Diced vegetables (such as bell peppers, spinach, or mushrooms)
- Salt and pepper to taste
- Cooking spray
- Preparation Procedures:

1. Preheat your Ninja Dual Zone Air Fryer to 175°C for about 5 minutes.
2. In a mixing bowl, whisk the eggs and milk until well combined. Season with salt and pepper according to your taste.
3. Prepare your muffin tin or silicone muffin cups by lightly greasing them with cooking spray.
4. Distribute the diced bacon or ham, vegetables, and shredded cheese evenly among the cups in the muffin tin.
5. Pour the egg mixture into each cup, filling them about 3/4 of the way. Leave a little room at the top as the quiches will puff up while cooking.
6. Place the muffin tin in the preheated air fryer basket.
7. Cook the quiches in the air fryer at 175°C for approximately 10-12 minutes or until set and the tops are lightly golden brown. You can check for doneness by inserting a toothpick into the center of a quiche. If it comes out clean, they are ready.
8. Carefully remove the muffin tin from the air fryer using oven mitts or tongs, as it will be hot. Let the quiches cool in the tin for a few minutes before removing them.
9. Use a butter knife or small spatula to gently loosen the quiches from the muffin cups. They should come out easily.
10. Serve the mini quiches warm as a delicious breakfast or brunch option.

Chapter 2 Lunch

Crispy Fried Asparagus Fries with Lemon Garlic Aioli

Serves 2 / Prep Time: 15 minutes / Cook Time: 15 minutes

- For the Asparagus Fries:
- 200g fresh asparagus spears, trimmed
- 1/2 cup all-purpose flour (60g)
- 2 large eggs, beaten
- 1 cup panko breadcrumbs (120g)
- 1/2 cup grated Parmesan cheese (60g)
- 1/2 teaspoon garlic powder
- Salt and pepper to taste
- Vegetable oil for frying
- For the Lemon Garlic Aioli:
- 1/2 cup mayonnaise (115g)
- 1 clove garlic, minced
- Zest and juice of 1 lemon
- 1 teaspoon Dijon mustard
- Salt and pepper to taste

1. Start by preparing the Lemon Garlic Aioli. In a small bowl, combine mayonnaise, minced garlic, lemon zest, lemon juice, Dijon mustard, salt, and pepper. Mix well and refrigerate the aioli while you prepare the asparagus fries.
2. In one bowl, place the all-purpose flour. In another bowl, add the beaten eggs. In a third bowl, mix the panko breadcrumbs, grated Parmesan cheese, garlic powder, salt, and pepper.
3. Dip each asparagus spear into the flour, then the beaten egg, and finally coat it with the breadcrumb mixture. Set them aside on a plate.
4. Preheat your deep fryer or a large, deep skillet with vegetable oil to 350°F (175°C).
5. Carefully place the coated asparagus fries into the hot oil and fry for about 2-3 minutes or until they are golden brown and crispy. Remove with a slotted spoon and place on paper towels to drain excess oil.
6. Serve the Crispy Fried Asparagus Fries with the Lemon Garlic Aioli for dipping.

Crispy Fried Eggplant Rollatini

Serves 2 / Prep Time: 20 minutes / Cook Time: 20 minutes

- For the Eggplant Rollatini:
- 1 large eggplant (about 500g)
- 1 cup ricotta cheese (240g)
- 1/2 cup grated Parmesan cheese (60g)
- 1/4 cup chopped fresh basil (15g)
- 1 clove garlic, minced
- Salt and pepper to taste
- 1 cup all-purpose flour (120g)
- 2 large eggs, beaten
- 1 cup breadcrumbs (120g)
- Vegetable oil for frying
- For the Marinara Sauce:
- 1 cup marinara sauce (240g)

1. Start by preparing the Eggplant Rollatini. Cut the eggplant into thin slices lengthwise, about 1/4 inch thick. Lay them out on paper towels and sprinkle with salt. Let them sit for about 15 minutes to release excess moisture, then pat them dry with paper towels.
2. In a bowl, combine ricotta cheese, grated Parmesan cheese, chopped fresh basil, minced garlic, salt, and pepper. Mix well.
3. Take each eggplant slice, spread a layer of the cheese mixture on it, then roll it up.
4. Dip each eggplant roll into all-purpose flour, then beaten eggs, and finally coat it with breadcrumbs. Place them on a plate.
5. Preheat your deep fryer or a large, deep skillet with vegetable oil to 350°F (175°C).
6. Carefully place the eggplant rolls into the hot oil and fry for about 3-4 minutes or until they are golden brown and crispy. Remove with a slotted spoon and place on paper towels to drain excess oil.
7. Warm the marinara sauce in a separate saucepan.

General Tso's Chicken

Serves 2 / Prep Time: 15 minutes / Cook Time: 15 minutes

- For the Chicken:
- 300g boneless, skinless chicken thighs, cut into bite-sized pieces
- 30g cornstarch
- 10g soy sauce
- 5g rice wine vinegar
- 5g ginger, minced
- 5g garlic, minced
- 2g red pepper flakes (adjust to taste)
- Cooking oil, for frying
- For the General Tso's Sauce:

- 40g sugar
- 30ml soy sauce
- 30ml rice wine vinegar
- 30ml chicken broth
- 5g cornstarch

1. In a bowl, mix together the cornstarch, soy sauce, rice wine vinegar, minced ginger, minced garlic, and red pepper flakes. Coat the chicken pieces with this mixture.
2. Preheat your Ninja Foodi Dual Zone Air Fryer to 375°F (190°C) using the "Air Fry" setting.
3. Lightly grease the air fryer basket with cooking oil.
4. Place the coated chicken pieces in the air fryer basket in a single layer.
5. Air fry for about 10-12 minutes, until the chicken is crispy and cooked through.
6. While the chicken is cooking, prepare the General Tso's sauce. In a saucepan, combine sugar, soy sauce, rice wine vinegar, chicken broth, and cornstarch. Cook over medium heat until the sauce thickens.
7. Once the chicken is done, toss it in the General Tso's sauce until well-coated.

Air Fryer Bacon-Wrapped Jalapeños

Serves 2 / Prep Time: 20 minutes / Cook Time: 10 minutes

- 6 large jalapeños
- 100g cream cheese
- 50g shredded cheddar cheese
- 6 slices of bacon
- 5g garlic powder
- Salt and black pepper to taste
- Toothpicks

1. Slice the jalapeños in half lengthwise and remove the seeds and membranes.
2. In a bowl, mix cream cheese, shredded cheddar cheese, garlic powder, salt, and black pepper.
3. Fill each jalapeño half with the cream cheese mixture.
4. Wrap each jalapeño with a slice of bacon and secure with a toothpick.
5. Preheat your Ninja Foodi Dual Zone Air Fryer to 375°F (190°C).
6. Place the bacon-wrapped jalapeños in the air fryer basket.
7. Air fry at 375°F (190°C) for 8-10 minutes, or until the bacon is crispy and the jalapeños are tender.

Air Fryer Stuffed Peppers

Serves 2 / Prep Time: 30 minutes / Cook Time: 20 minutes

- 2 large bell peppers, halved and cleaned
- 150g ground beef
- 100g cooked rice
- 50g diced tomatoes
- 50g diced onions
- 30g shredded cheddar cheese
- 5g garlic powder
- Salt and black pepper to taste
- Cooking spray

1. In a skillet, cook ground beef and diced onions until the beef is browned. Drain any excess fat.
2. In a bowl, mix the cooked beef, cooked rice, diced tomatoes, garlic powder, salt, and black pepper.
3. Stuff each bell pepper half with the beef and rice mixture.
4. Sprinkle shredded cheddar cheese on top of each stuffed pepper.
5. Preheat your Ninja Foodi Dual Zone Air Fryer to 375°F (190°C).
6. Spray the air fryer basket with cooking spray and place the stuffed peppers inside.
7. Air fry at 375°F (190°C) for 18-20 minutes, or until the peppers are tender and the cheese is melted and bubbly.

Air Fryer Stuffed Poblano Peppers

Serves 2 / Prep Time: 30 minutes / Cook Time: 20 minutes

- 2 large poblano peppers
- 200g ground beef
- 100g cooked rice
- 50g black beans, drained and rinsed
- 50g diced tomatoes
- 30g shredded cheddar cheese
- 5g chili powder
- 5g cumin
- Salt and black pepper to taste
- Cooking spray

1. Roast the poblano peppers in the air fryer at 375°F (190°C) for 5-7 minutes, turning occasionally, until the skin is blistered. Remove and let them cool.
2. In a skillet, cook ground beef until browned. Drain any excess fat.
3. In a bowl, mix cooked beef, cooked rice, black beans, diced tomatoes, chili powder, cumin, salt, and black pepper.
4. Carefully peel the roasted poblano peppers, make a small slit, and stuff them with the beef and rice mixture.
5. Sprinkle shredded cheddar cheese on top of each stuffed pepper.

6. Preheat your Ninja Foodi Dual Zone Air Fryer to 375°F (190°C).
7. Spray the air fryer basket with cooking spray and place the stuffed poblano peppers inside.
8. Air fry at 375°F (190°C) for 18-20 minutes, or until the peppers are tender and the cheese is melted and bubbly.

Fried Zucchini Roll-Ups with Ricotta and Spinach

Serves 2 / Prep Time: 30 minutes / Cook Time: 15 minutes

- For Zucchini Roll-Ups:
- 2 large zucchini, sliced into thin strips
- 150g ricotta cheese
- 100g chopped spinach
- 5g minced garlic
- 5g dried oregano
- Salt and black pepper to taste
- Cooking oil for frying
- For Tomato Sauce:
- 200g tomato sauce
- 5g dried basil
- 5g dried thyme
- Salt and black pepper to taste

1. In a bowl, mix ricotta cheese, chopped spinach, minced garlic, dried oregano, salt, and black pepper.
2. Lay out the zucchini strips and spread the ricotta-spinach mixture on each strip. Roll them up.
3. In a separate bowl, mix tomato sauce, dried basil, dried thyme, salt, and black pepper. Set aside.
4. Preheat your Ninja Foodi Dual Zone Air Fryer to 375°F (190°C).
5. Fill one zone with cooking oil and preheat it for frying.
6. Once the oil is hot, carefully place the zucchini roll-ups in the oil and fry for 2-3 minutes on each side until they are golden brown.
7. Place the fried roll-ups on paper towels to remove excess oil.
8. Serve the zucchini roll-ups with the tomato sauce.

Air Fryer Chicken Cordon Bleu

Serves 2 / Prep Time: 20 minutes / Cook Time: 20 minutes

- 2 boneless, skinless chicken breasts (about 200g each)
- 100g ham slices
- 50g Swiss cheese slices
- 30g all-purpose flour
- 1 egg, beaten
- 100g breadcrumbs
- 10g olive oil
- Salt and black pepper to taste

1. Preheat your Ninja Foodi Dual Zone Air Fryer to 375°F (190°C) on the "Air Fry" setting.
2. Season the chicken breasts with salt and black pepper.
3. Lay out a chicken breast, top with a slice of ham and a slice of Swiss cheese, then roll up and secure with toothpicks.
4. Set up three shallow bowls with the flour in one, beaten egg in another, and breadcrumbs in the third.
5. Dredge each chicken roll in the flour, then dip in the beaten egg, and coat with breadcrumbs.
6. Place the chicken rolls in the air fryer basket.
7. Drizzle the olive oil over the chicken rolls.
8. Air fry at 375°F (190°C) for about 18-20 minutes, or until the chicken is cooked through and the coating is golden brown and crispy.
9. Remove the toothpicks before serving.
10. Serve your Chicken Cordon Bleu hot.

Air Fryer Coquilles Saint-Jacques

Serves 2 / Prep Time: 20 minutes / Cook Time: 15 minutes

- 200g scallops
- 100g button mushrooms, sliced
- 50g butter
- 50g heavy cream
- 20g white wine
- 10g bread crumbs
- 10g grated Parmesan cheese
- Salt and black pepper to taste
- Fresh parsley, chopped (for garnish)

1. Preheat your Ninja Foodi Dual Zone Air Fryer to 375°F (190°C) on the "Air Fry" setting.
2. In a skillet, sauté the sliced mushrooms in butter until they are tender. Add the white wine and heavy cream, then simmer until the sauce thickens.
3. Season the scallops with salt and black pepper.
4. Place the scallops in one of the air fryer zones, ensuring they are not crowded.
5. In the other zone, air fry the bread crumbs and Parmesan cheese until they are lightly browned.
6. Once the scallops are done, remove them from the air fryer.
7. Pour the mushroom and cream sauce over the scallops.
8. Top the scallops with the toasted bread crumbs and

Parmesan mixture.
9. Garnish with chopped fresh parsley.
10. Serve your Coquilles Saint-Jacques hot and enjoy.

Air Fryer Chicken Parmesan

Serves 2 / Prep Time: 15 minutes / Cook Time: 20 minutes

- 2 boneless, skinless chicken breasts (about 300g each)
- 100g all-purpose flour
- 2 eggs, beaten
- 150g breadcrumbs
- 150g marinara sauce
- 100g shredded mozzarella cheese
- 5g dried basil
- 5g dried oregano
- 5g garlic powder
- Salt and black pepper to taste
- Cooking spray

1. Season the chicken breasts with salt, black pepper, dried basil, dried oregano, and garlic powder.
2. Dredge the chicken in flour, dip it in beaten eggs, and coat with breadcrumbs.
3. Preheat your Ninja Foodi Dual Zone Air Fryer to 375°F (190°C).
4. Spray the chicken breasts with cooking spray and place them in the air fryer basket.
5. Air fry at 375°F (190°C) for 18-20 minutes, or until the chicken is cooked through and the coating is crispy.
6. In the last 3 minutes of cooking, add marinara sauce and shredded mozzarella on top of the chicken to melt and bubble.

Air Fryer Beef and Broccoli

Serves 2 / Prep Time: 20 minutes / Cook Time: 15 minutes

- 300g beef sirloin or flank steak, thinly sliced
- 200g broccoli florets
- 5g garlic, minced
- 5g ginger, minced
- 30g soy sauce
- 10g oyster sauce
- 10g brown sugar
- 10g cornstarch
- 10g sesame oil
- Cooking spray

1. In a bowl, mix the soy sauce, oyster sauce, brown sugar, cornstarch, and sesame oil to make the sauce.
2. Toss the sliced beef with the minced garlic and ginger.
3. Preheat your Ninja Foodi Dual Zone Air Fryer to 375°F (190°C).
4. Place the broccoli in one zone of the air fryer and the beef in the other zone. Spray with cooking spray.
5. Air fry at 375°F (190°C) for 10-12 minutes, stirring once, until the beef is cooked and the broccoli is tender.
6. In the last 2 minutes, pour the sauce over the beef and cook until the sauce thickens.

Fried Chicken Parmesan Sliders

Serves 2 / Prep Time: 20 minutes / Cook Time: 15 minutes

- 2 chicken breasts (about 200g each)
- 100g all-purpose flour
- 2 eggs, beaten
- 150g breadcrumbs
- 50g marinara sauce
- 100g shredded mozzarella cheese
- 4 mini slider buns
- 5g dried basil
- 5g dried oregano
- 5g garlic powder
- Salt and black pepper to taste
- Cooking spray

1. Season the chicken breasts with salt, black pepper, dried basil, dried oregano, and garlic powder.
2. Dredge the chicken in flour, dip it in beaten eggs, and coat with breadcrumbs.
3. Preheat your Ninja Foodi Dual Zone Air Fryer to 375°F (190°C).
4. Spray the chicken breasts with cooking spray and place them in the air fryer basket.
5. Air fry at 375°F (190°C) for 12-15 minutes, or until the chicken is cooked through and the coating is crispy.
6. In the last 2 minutes of cooking, add marinara sauce and shredded mozzarella on top of each chicken breast to melt and bubble.
7. Toast the mini slider buns in the air fryer for 1-2 minutes.
8. Place each chicken breast on a slider bun to create the sliders.

Crispy Fried Sweet Potato Fritters with Spicy Aioli

Serves 2 / Prep Time: 20 minutes / Cook Time: 15 minutes

- For Sweet Potato Fritters:
- 300g sweet potatoes, peeled and grated

- 50g all-purpose flour
- 1 egg
- 5g baking powder
- 5g paprika
- Salt and pepper to taste
- Cooking oil for frying
- For Spicy Aioli:
- 50g mayonnaise
- 10g hot sauce
- 5g minced garlic
- Salt and pepper to taste

1. In a bowl, mix grated sweet potatoes, all-purpose flour, egg, baking powder, paprika, salt, and pepper until well combined.
2. Shape the mixture into small fritters.
3. In another bowl, combine mayonnaise, hot sauce, minced garlic, salt, and pepper. Mix well and set aside.
4. Preheat your Ninja Foodi Dual Zone Air Fryer to 375°F (190°C).
5. Fill one zone with cooking oil and preheat it for frying.
6. Once the oil is hot, carefully place the sweet potato fritters in the oil and fry for 2-3 minutes on each side until they are golden brown and crispy.
7. Place the fried fritters on paper towels to remove excess oil.
8. Serve the sweet potato fritters with the spicy aioli on the side.

Air Fryer Beef Bourguignon Pot Pie

Serves 2 / Prep Time: 30 minutes / Cook Time: 25 minutes

- 300g beef stew meat, cubed
- 200g mushrooms, quartered
- 100g pearl onions
- 2 garlic cloves, minced
- 200ml red wine
- 200ml beef broth
- 15ml olive oil
- 5g all-purpose flour
- 2g dried thyme
- 2g dried rosemary
- Salt and pepper, to taste
- 1 sheet of puff pastry dough

1. Preheat your Ninja Foodi Dual Zone Air Fryer to 375°F (190°C) on the "Bake/Roast" setting.
2. Season the beef stew meat with salt, pepper, and all-purpose flour, ensuring the meat is coated.
3. In a bowl, mix dried thyme and dried rosemary with olive oil.
4. In one air fryer zone, sear the beef stew meat until browned on all sides. Remove and set aside.
5. In the same air fryer zone, add quartered mushrooms and pearl onions. Sauté until they start to brown.
6. Add minced garlic and cook for a minute.
7. Return the beef stew meat to the air fryer.
8. Pour in red wine and beef broth.
9. Air fry at 375°F (190°C) for about 1 hour, stirring occasionally, until the beef is tender and the sauce thickens.
10. In the other air fryer zone, cut the puff pastry dough into two circles that fit your serving dishes.
11. Place the circles on a parchment paper-lined tray.
12. Air fry at 375°F (190°C) for about 12-15 minutes, or until the pastry is puffed and golden.
13. Serve your Beef Bourguignon Filling in individual dishes, and top with the puff pastry.
14. Enjoy your Air Fryer Beef Bourguignon Pot Pie!

Crispy Fried Artichoke Salad with Lemon Parmesan Dressing

Serves 2 / Prep Time: 20 minutes / Cook Time: 10 minutes

- For Crispy Fried Artichokes:
- 200g canned artichoke hearts, drained and patted dry
- 50g all-purpose flour
- 1 egg, beaten
- 100g breadcrumbs
- Cooking oil for frying
- Salt and black pepper to taste
- For Lemon Parmesan Dressing:
- 30g grated Parmesan cheese
- Juice of 1 lemon
- 5g minced garlic
- 5g Dijon mustard
- 10g olive oil
- Salt and black pepper to taste
- For Salad:
- 150g mixed greens (e. g. , arugula, spinach, lettuce)
- 50g cherry tomatoes, halved
- 30g red onion, thinly sliced

1. Dredge artichoke hearts in flour, dip them in beaten egg, and coat with breadcrumbs.
2. In a bowl, whisk together Parmesan cheese, lemon juice, minced garlic, Dijon mustard, olive oil, salt, and black pepper.
3. Preheat your Ninja Foodi Dual Zone Air Fryer to 375°F (190°C).
4. Fill one zone with cooking oil and preheat it for frying.

5. Once the oil is hot, carefully place the breaded artichoke hearts in the oil and fry for 2-3 minutes on each side until they are golden brown.
6. Place the fried artichoke hearts on paper towels to remove excess oil.
7. In a large bowl, toss mixed greens, cherry tomatoes, and red onion with the Lemon Parmesan Dressing.
8. Arrange the crispy fried artichoke hearts on top of the salad.

Air Fryer Beef Daube Provençal

Serves 2 / Prep Time: 20 minutes / Cook Time: 30 minutes
- 400g beef stew meat, cut into cubes
- 100g red wine
- 200g canned diced tomatoes
- 100g carrots, sliced
- 100g onions, chopped
- 50g celery, chopped
- 2 cloves garlic, minced
- 10g olive oil
- 5g tomato paste
- 5g Herbes de Provence
- Salt and black pepper to taste

1. In a bowl, marinate the beef cubes with red wine, Herbes de Provence, minced garlic, salt, and black pepper. Let it sit for at least 10 minutes.
2. In another bowl, mix the tomato paste with the canned diced tomatoes.
3. Preheat your Ninja Foodi Dual Zone Air Fryer to 350°F (180°C) on the "Air Fry" setting.
4. In one of the air fryer zones, heat the olive oil using the "Sear/Sauté" function. Add the marinated beef cubes and sear them until browned, then remove and set aside.
5. In the same zone, add the chopped onions, carrots, and celery. Sauté until they start to soften.
6. Return the beef to the zone and pour in the tomato paste and diced tomato mixture.
7. Cook at 350°F (180°C) for 30 minutes, occasionally stirring. If it gets too dry, you can add a little water.
8. Serve your Beef Daube Provençal with a side of crusty bread and enjoy.

Air Fryer Duck à l'Orange with Grand Marnier Sauce

Serves 2 / Prep Time: 15 minutes / Cook Time: 25 minutes
- 2 duck breasts (about 300g each)
- 100g orange juice
- 50g Grand Marnier (orange liqueur)
- 10g brown sugar
- 5g cornstarch
- Salt and black pepper to taste

1. Score the duck breasts' skin in a crisscross pattern, being careful not to cut into the meat. Season with salt and black pepper.
2. In a small bowl, mix the orange juice, Grand Marnier, brown sugar, and cornstarch to create the sauce.
3. Preheat your Ninja Foodi Dual Zone Air Fryer to 375°F (190°C) on the "Roast" setting.
4. Place the duck breasts skin-side down in the air fryer basket and air fry at 375°F (190°C) for 10 minutes.
5. Flip the duck breasts and air fry for an additional 10-15 minutes or until the internal temperature reaches 165°F (74°C) for medium-rare or adjust to your desired doneness.
6. While the duck is cooking, pour the sauce into a saucepan and heat over low heat, stirring until it thickens.
7. Serve the duck breasts with the Grand Marnier sauce and enjoy.

Fried Pickle Potato Skins with Bacon and Cheddar

Serves 2 / Prep Time: 20 minutes / Cook Time: 15 minutes
- For the Potato Skins:
- 2 large russet potatoes (about 300g each)
- 10g vegetable oil
- Salt and black pepper to taste
- 60g shredded cheddar cheese
- 30g bacon bits
- For the Fried Pickles:
- 100g dill pickle slices
- 50g all-purpose flour
- 1 egg
- 30g Panko breadcrumbs
- 5g paprika
- Vegetable oil for frying
- For Dipping:
- 30g sour cream

1. Preheat your Ninja Foodi Dual Zone Air Fryer to 375°F (190°C) on the "Air Fry" setting.
2. Scrub and wash the russet potatoes, then dry them.
3. In a bowl, coat the potatoes with vegetable oil and season with salt and black pepper.
4. Using a fork, pierce the potatoes in several places.
5. In a separate bowl, prepare the fried pickles.

Dredge the pickle slices in flour, dip them in beaten egg, and coat them in Panko breadcrumbs mixed with paprika.
6. Place the prepared potatoes in one air fryer zone.
7. Air fry at 375°F (190°C) for about 15 minutes, or until the potatoes are cooked through and the skins are crispy.
8. Remove the potatoes from the air fryer, and once they're cool enough to handle, cut them in half lengthwise.
9. Scoop out some of the flesh to create potato skins.
10. Return the potato skins to the air fryer basket, skin side up.
11. Sprinkle shredded cheddar cheese and bacon bits over the potato skins.
12. Air fry for an additional 5 minutes, or until the cheese is melted and bubbly.
13. In the other air fryer zone, place the coated pickle slices.
14. Air fry at 375°F (190°C) for about 4-5 minutes, turning them once, until they are golden and crispy.
15. Serve the fried pickle potato skins with a side of sour cream for dipping.
16. Enjoy your Fried Pickle Potato Skins with Bacon and Cheddar!

Air Fryer Chicken Florentine

Serves 2 / Prep Time: 15 minutes / Cook Time: 15 minutes

- 2 boneless, skinless chicken breasts (about 300g each)
- 100g fresh spinach, chopped
- 100g ricotta cheese
- 10g grated Parmesan cheese
- 2 cloves garlic, minced
- 5g olive oil
- Salt and black pepper to taste

1. Preheat your Ninja Foodi Dual Zone Air Fryer to 375°F (190°C) on the "Air Fry" setting.
2. In a bowl, combine the chopped spinach, ricotta cheese, grated Parmesan cheese, minced garlic, salt, and black pepper.
3. Cut a pocket into each chicken breast without cutting all the way through.
4. Stuff each chicken breast with the spinach and cheese mixture.
5. Brush the stuffed chicken breasts with olive oil.
6. Place the chicken breasts in the air fryer basket and air fry at 375°F (190°C) for about 15 minutes, or until the internal temperature reaches 165°F (74°C) and the chicken is golden brown and cooked through.
7. Serve your Chicken Florentine hot and enjoy.

Air Fryer Duck Confit

Serves 2 / Prep Time: 20 minutes / Cook Time: 45 minutes

- 2 duck leg quarters (about 400g each)
- 5g salt
- 2g black pepper
- 2g thyme
- 2g rosemary
- 2 cloves garlic, minced

1. Preheat your Ninja Foodi Dual Zone Air Fryer to 375°F (190°C) on the "Roast" setting.
2. Season the duck leg quarters with salt, black pepper, thyme, rosemary, and minced garlic. Make sure to rub the seasonings into the duck legs.
3. Place the seasoned duck leg quarters in the air fryer basket, skin side down.
4. Air fry at 375°F (190°C) for 15 minutes, then reduce the temperature to 325°F (165°C) and continue to air fry for an additional 30 minutes, or until the duck is crispy and the internal temperature reaches 165°F (74°C).
5. Serve your Duck Confit hot, and enjoy this flavorful dish.

Arancini (Italian Rice Balls)

Serves 2 / Prep Time: 30 minutes / Cook Time: 20 minutes

- 300g cooked and cooled Arborio rice
- 100g mozzarella cheese, cut into small cubes
- 2 large eggs
- 50g grated Parmesan cheese
- 100g breadcrumbs
- 1/2 tsp salt
- 1/4 tsp black pepper
- 1/2 tsp dried oregano
- Cooking spray
- Marinara sauce for dipping (optional)

1. In a mixing bowl, combine the cooked Arborio rice, grated Parmesan cheese, salt, black pepper, and dried oregano.
2. Beat the eggs in a separate bowl.
3. Take a small portion of the rice mixture, flatten it in your hand, place a cube of mozzarella cheese in the center, and form it into a ball.
4. Dip each rice ball into the beaten eggs and then roll it in breadcrumbs to coat evenly.
5. Place the prepared Arancini on a plate.
6. Preheat the Ninja Foodi Dual Zone Air Fryer to 375°F (190°C) using the "Air Fry" setting.
7. Place the Arancini in the Dual Zone Air Fryer

basket, ensuring they are in a single layer and not overcrowded.
8. Spray the Arancini with cooking spray.
9. Set the Dual Zone Air Fryer to Air Fry at 375°F (190°C) for 15-20 minutes or until the Arancini are golden brown and the cheese inside is melted.
10. Serve hot with marinara sauce for dipping, if desired.

Fried Chicken and Biscuit Sliders with Honey Butter

Serves 2 / Prep Time: 20 minutes / Cook Time: 15 minutes

- For the Fried Chicken:
- 200g boneless, skinless chicken breasts
- 100g buttermilk
- 100g all-purpose flour
- 5g paprika
- 5g garlic powder
- 5g onion powder
- Salt and black pepper to taste
- Vegetable oil for frying
- For the Biscuits:
- 2 small biscuits (about 100g each)
- For the Honey Butter:
- 30g butter, softened
- 20g honey

1. Preheat your Ninja Foodi Dual Zone Air Fryer to 375°F (190°C) on the "Air Fry" setting.
2. Slice the chicken breasts into slider-sized pieces and place them in a bowl. Pour the buttermilk over the chicken and let it marinate for about 15 minutes.
3. In a separate bowl, mix the flour, paprika, garlic powder, onion powder, salt, and black pepper.
4. In another small bowl, combine the softened butter and honey to make the honey butter.
5. In one air fryer zone, coat the marinated chicken pieces with the seasoned flour mixture.
6. Place the chicken pieces in the air fryer basket and air fry at 375°F (190°C) for about 12-15 minutes, turning them halfway through, until they are crispy and cooked through.
7. In the other air fryer zone, place the biscuits and air fry at 375°F (190°C) for about 8-10 minutes until they are golden brown and cooked.
8. Split the biscuits in half.
9. Assemble your sliders by placing the fried chicken on the biscuit bottoms and topping with honey butter.
10. Place the biscuit tops on the sliders.
11. Serve your Fried Chicken and Biscuit Sliders hot and enjoy!

Air Fryer Chicken and Mushroom Vol-au-Vent

Serves 2 / Prep Time: 20 minutes / Cook Time: 15 minutes

- For the Filling:
- 200g chicken breast, diced
- 100g mushrooms, sliced
- 30g butter
- 30g all-purpose flour
- 200ml chicken broth
- 60ml heavy cream
- 5g fresh thyme, chopped
- Salt and black pepper to taste
- For the Vol-au-Vent:
- 2 sheets of puff pastry, thawed
- 1 egg, beaten (for egg wash)

1. Preheat your Ninja Foodi Dual Zone Air Fryer to 375°F (190°C) on the "Air Fry" setting.
2. In a skillet, melt the butter and sauté the diced chicken until it's no longer pink.
3. Add the sliced mushrooms and fresh thyme, cooking until the mushrooms are tender.
4. Stir in the all-purpose flour and cook for a minute or two to create a roux.
5. Slowly whisk in the chicken broth and heavy cream, continuing to stir until the sauce thickens. Season with salt and black pepper
6. Cut a circle from the center of each puff pastry sheet to create a border, and remove the center circle.
7. In one air fryer zone, place the puff pastry sheets with the borders.
8. Air fry at 375°F (190°C) for about 5-7 minutes, or until they are golden and puffed up.
9. In the other air fryer zone, place the prepared chicken and mushroom filling.
10. Air fry at 375°F (190°C) for about 10 minutes, or until the filling is hot and bubbly.
11. Spoon the filling into the center of the puff pastry vol-au-vents.
12. Serve your Air Fryer Chicken and Mushroom Vol-au-Vent!

Air Fryer Porcini Mushroom Risotto

Serves 2 / Prep Time: 10 minutes / Cook Time: 20 minutes

- 150g Arborio rice
- 10g dried porcini mushrooms

- 100g mushrooms, sliced
- 30g shallots, chopped
- 2 garlic cloves, minced
- 30ml white wine
- 400ml chicken or vegetable broth
- 15ml olive oil
- 15g grated Parmesan cheese
- Salt and pepper, to taste
- Fresh parsley, chopped (for garnish)

1. Preheat your Ninja Foodi Dual Zone Air Fryer to 360°F (180°C) on the "Air Fry" setting.
2. Soak the dried porcini mushrooms in hot water for about 10 minutes. Drain and chop them.
3. In a bowl, mix the sliced mushrooms with olive oil, salt, and pepper.
4. In one air fryer zone, place the sliced mushrooms.
5. Air fry at 360°F (180°C) for about 10-12 minutes, or until they are golden brown and crispy.
6. In the other air fryer zone, sauté the chopped shallots and minced garlic until translucent.
7. Add Arborio rice and cook for a couple of minutes, stirring.
8. Pour in white wine and let it evaporate.
9. Add chopped porcini mushrooms.
10. Gradually add chicken or vegetable broth, stirring constantly until the rice is creamy and cooked to your desired level of doneness.
11. Stir in grated Parmesan cheese and the air-fried mushrooms.
12. Season with salt and pepper.
13. Garnish with chopped fresh parsley.
14. Serve your Air Fryer Porcini Mushroom Risotto!

Air Fryer Chicken Piccata

Serves 2 / Prep Time: 15 minutes / Cook Time: 20 minutes

- 2 boneless, skinless chicken breasts (about 200g each)
- 100g all-purpose flour
- 10g olive oil
- 100g chicken broth
- 60g fresh lemon juice
- 20g capers
- 10g butter
- Salt and black pepper to taste
- Fresh parsley, chopped (for garnish)

1. Preheat your Ninja Foodi Dual Zone Air Fryer to 375°F (190°C) on the "Air Fry" setting.
2. Season the chicken breasts with salt and black pepper.
3. Dredge the chicken breasts in flour, shaking off the excess.
4. Place the chicken breasts in the air fryer basket and air fry at 375°F (190°C) for about 15-20 minutes, turning them halfway through, until they reach an internal temperature of 165°F (74°C) and are golden brown.
5. While the chicken is cooking, heat the olive oil in a skillet. Add the capers, lemon juice, chicken broth, and butter. Cook until the sauce thickens, stirring occasionally.
6. Pour the piccata sauce over the cooked chicken breasts.
7. Garnish with chopped fresh parsley.
8. Serve your Chicken Piccata hot and enjoy.

Air Fryer Paella

Serves 2 / Prep Time: 20 minutes / Cook Time: 25 minutes

- 200g chicken thighs, boneless and diced
- 200g jumbo shrimp, peeled and deveined
- 100g Spanish chorizo, sliced
- 100g bell peppers, diced
- 100g onion, diced
- 100g Arborio rice
- 2 cloves garlic, minced
- 10g smoked paprika
- 5g saffron threads (optional for color and flavor)
- 400g chicken broth
- 20g olive oil
- Salt and black pepper to taste
- Lemon wedges and fresh parsley for garnish

1. Preheat your Ninja Foodi Dual Zone Air Fryer to 375°F (190°C) on the "Air Fry" setting.
2. In a bowl, combine the diced chicken thighs with smoked paprika, minced garlic, salt, and black pepper. Toss to coat.
3. In one air fryer zone, add the marinated chicken and Spanish chorizo. Air fry at 375°F (190°C) for about 8-10 minutes, or until the chicken is browned and the chorizo is crispy. Remove and set aside.
4. In the other zone, add olive oil, bell peppers, and onions. Air fry for about 5 minutes, or until they start to soften.
5. Add the Arborio rice to the peppers and onions, and continue to air fry for another 2-3 minutes until the rice is translucent.
6. Pour in the chicken broth and add saffron threads, if using. Stir to combine.
7. Return the cooked chicken and chorizo to the air fryer, along with the jumbo shrimp.
8. Air fry at 375°F (190°C) for another 8-10 minutes, or until the rice is cooked and the shrimp turn pink.

9. Garnish with fresh parsley and lemon wedges before serving.
10. Serve your Paella hot and enjoy the flavors of Spain!

Air Fryer Chicken Kiev

Serves 2 / Prep Time: 20 minutes / Cook Time: 20 minutes

- 2 boneless, skinless chicken breasts (about 200g each)
- 50g unsalted butter, softened
- 5g fresh parsley, chopped
- 5g fresh dill, chopped
- 2 cloves garlic, minced
- 10g lemon juice
- 30g all-purpose flour
- 1 large egg
- 60g breadcrumbs
- 10g olive oil
- Salt and black pepper to taste

1. Preheat your Ninja Foodi Dual Zone Air Fryer to 375°F (190°C) on the "Air Fry" setting.
2. In a bowl, combine the softened butter, chopped fresh parsley, chopped fresh dill, minced garlic, lemon juice, salt, and black pepper.
3. Carefully butterfly each chicken breast by slicing it horizontally, then spread the herb butter mixture inside each breast.
4. Dredge each stuffed chicken breast in flour, shaking off the excess.
5. Dip the floured chicken breasts into a beaten egg.
6. Coat the chicken breasts with breadcrumbs, pressing the breadcrumbs to adhere.
7. Brush the chicken breasts with olive oil.
8. Place the chicken breasts in the air fryer basket and air fry at 375°F (190°C) for about 20 minutes, turning them halfway through, until they are golden brown and reach an internal temperature of 165°F (74°C).
9. Serve your Chicken Kiev hot, and enjoy this classic dish.

Air Fryer Veal Piccata

Serves 2 / Prep Time: 15 minutes / Cook Time: 20 minutes

- 2 veal cutlets (about 150g each)
- 30g all-purpose flour
- 10g olive oil
- 60g chicken broth
- 40g lemon juice
- 20g capers
- 20g butter
- Salt and black pepper to taste
- Fresh parsley, chopped (for garnish)

1. Preheat your Ninja Foodi Dual Zone Air Fryer to 375°F (190°C) on the "Air Fry" setting.
2. Season the veal cutlets with salt and black pepper.
3. Dredge each cutlet in flour, shaking off the excess.
4. Place the veal cutlets in the air fryer basket.
5. Air fry at 375°F (190°C) for about 10-15 minutes, turning them halfway through, until they are golden brown and cooked to your preferred level of doneness.
6. In a skillet, heat the olive oil. Add the capers, lemon juice, chicken broth, and butter. Cook until the sauce thickens, stirring occasionally.
7. Pour the piccata sauce over the cooked veal cutlets.
8. Garnish with chopped fresh parsley.
9. Serve your Veal Piccata hot and enjoy this delicious dish.

Air Fryer Coq au Vin

Serves 2 / Prep Time: 20 minutes / Cook Time: 25 minutes

- 4 bone-in, skin-on chicken thighs (about 250g each)
- 100g bacon, diced
- 100g pearl onions, peeled
- 200g mushrooms, sliced
- 2 cloves garlic, minced
- 100g red wine
- 200g chicken broth
- 10g all-purpose flour
- 10g butter
- 5g fresh thyme
- Salt and black pepper to taste

1. Preheat your Ninja Foodi Dual Zone Air Fryer to 375°F (190°C) on the "Air Fry" setting.
2. In a bowl, mix the chicken thighs with salt, black pepper, and flour until they are coated.
3. In a separate bowl, combine the red wine, chicken broth, and fresh thyme.
4. Place the bacon in one of the air fryer zones and air fry at 375°F (190°C) until crispy. Remove and set aside.
5. In the same zone, sear the chicken thighs, skin side down, until they are browned and crispy. Turn the thighs over and sear for a few more minutes. Remove and set aside.
6. In the other zone, add the butter, pearl onions, and sliced mushrooms. Sauté until they are slightly tender.

7. Add the minced garlic and sauté for another minute.
8. Return the chicken and bacon to the pan, and pour the wine and chicken broth mixture over everything.
9. Air fry at 375°F (190°C) for about 15-20 minutes until the chicken is cooked through and the sauce thickens.
10. Serve your Coq au Vin hot, and enjoy this classic French dish.

Air Fryer Truffle Risotto

Serves 2 / Prep Time: 10 minutes / Cook Time: 25 minutes

- 150g Arborio rice
- 1 small onion, finely chopped
- 2 cloves garlic, minced
- 100g dry white wine
- 400g chicken or vegetable broth
- 20g truffle oil
- 30g grated Parmesan cheese
- Salt and black pepper to taste
- Chopped fresh chives (for garnish)

1. Preheat your Ninja Foodi Dual Zone Air Fryer to 350°F (180°C) on the "Air Fry" setting.
2. In one zone, heat the chicken or vegetable broth.
3. In the other zone, sauté the finely chopped onion and minced garlic with truffle oil until the onion becomes translucent.
4. Add the Arborio rice and stir to coat with the truffle oil.
5. Pour in the white wine and cook until it is absorbed by the rice.
6. Begin adding the heated broth one ladle at a time, stirring constantly and allowing the liquid to be absorbed before adding more. Continue until the rice is creamy and al dente, which should take about 18-20 minutes.
7. Stir in the grated Parmesan cheese, salt, and black pepper.
8. Serve your Truffle Risotto hot, garnished with chopped fresh chives.

Air Fryer Chicken Alfredo

Serves 2 / Prep Time: 15 minutes / Cook Time: 20 minutes

- 200g fettuccine pasta
- 2 boneless, skinless chicken breasts (about 200g each)
- 20g olive oil
- 200g heavy cream
- 20g butter
- 20g grated Parmesan cheese
- 2 cloves garlic, minced
- 5g Italian seasoning
- Salt and black pepper to taste
- Fresh parsley, chopped (for garnish)

1. Preheat your Ninja Foodi Dual Zone Air Fryer to 375°F (190°C) on the "Air Fry" setting.
2. Cook the fettuccine pasta according to the package instructions. Drain and set aside.
3. Season the chicken breasts with salt, black pepper, and Italian seasoning.
4. In one of the air fryer zones, heat the olive oil. Place the seasoned chicken breasts and air fry at 375°F (190°C) for about 10-15 minutes, turning them halfway through, until they are browned and cooked through.
5. In the other zone, melt the butter. Add minced garlic and sauté for about a minute. Stir in the heavy cream and grated Parmesan cheese, and cook until the sauce thickens.
6. Slice the cooked chicken breasts into strips and add them to the sauce.
7. Serve the chicken and Alfredo sauce over the cooked fettuccine pasta.
8. Garnish with chopped fresh parsley.
9. Enjoy your Chicken Alfredo.

Chapter 3 Dinner

Fried Cheese-Stuffed Portobello Mushrooms

Serves 2 / Prep Time: 20 minutes / Cook Time: 12 minutes

- 2 large Portobello mushrooms
- 100g mozzarella cheese, shredded
- 1/4 cup grated Parmesan cheese (30g)
- 2 cloves garlic, minced
- 2 tablespoons fresh parsley, chopped
- Salt and black pepper to taste
- Olive oil for brushing

1. Preheat your Ninja Foodi Dual Zone Air Fryer to 375°F (190°C).
2. Carefully remove the stems from the Portobello mushrooms and scoop out the gills to create a hollow space for the stuffing.
3. In a bowl, mix together mozzarella cheese, grated Parmesan cheese, minced garlic, chopped fresh parsley, salt, and black pepper.
4. Stuff the mushrooms with the cheese mixture.
5. Cooking the Cheese-Stuffed Portobello Mushrooms:
6. Brush the stuffed Portobello mushrooms with a little olive oil to help them crisp up in the air fryer.
7. Place the mushrooms in the air fryer basket.
8. Air fry at 375°F (190°C) for about 10-12 minutes until the mushrooms are tender, and the cheese is melted and bubbly.

Crispy Fried Okra with Cajun Remoulade

Serves 2 / Prep Time: 15 minutes / Cook Time: 15 minutes

- For the Crispy Fried Okra:
- 200g fresh okra, sliced into 1-inch pieces
- 1/2 cup buttermilk (120g)
- 1 cup cornmeal (120g)
- 1/2 cup all-purpose flour (60g)
- 1/2 teaspoon Cajun seasoning
- 1/2 teaspoon salt
- Vegetable oil for frying
- For the Cajun Remoulade:
- 1/2 cup mayonnaise (115g)
- 1 tablespoon Dijon mustard
- 1 tablespoon lemon juice
- 1 teaspoon Cajun seasoning
- 1 clove garlic, minced
- Salt and pepper to taste

1. In a bowl, combine buttermilk and sliced okra. Allow the okra to soak in the buttermilk for 10-15 minutes.
2. In another bowl, mix together cornmeal, all-purpose flour, Cajun seasoning, and salt.
3. In a separate bowl, prepare the Cajun Remoulade by mixing mayonnaise, Dijon mustard, lemon juice, Cajun seasoning, minced garlic, salt, and pepper. Refrigerate until needed.
4. Preheat your deep fryer or a large, deep skillet with vegetable oil to 350°F (175°C).
5. Remove the okra from the buttermilk, allowing any excess to drip off.
6. Dredge the okra pieces in the cornmeal-flour mixture, ensuring they are well coated.
7. Carefully place the coated okra into the hot oil and fry for about 2-3 minutes or until they are golden brown and crispy. Remove with a slotted spoon and place on paper towels to drain excess oil.
8. Serve the Crispy Fried Okra with the Cajun Remoulade for dipping.

Air Fryer Steak Fajitas

Serves 2 / Prep Time: 15 minutes / Cook Time: 15 minutes

- 300g beef sirloin steak, thinly sliced
- 1 red bell pepper, thinly sliced
- 1 green bell pepper, thinly sliced
- 1 red onion, thinly sliced
- 2 tablespoons olive oil
- 1 tablespoon fajita seasoning
- 2 small tortillas (corn or flour)
- Sour cream, guacamole, and salsa for serving

1. In a bowl, combine the sliced beef, sliced bell peppers, sliced red onion, olive oil, and fajita seasoning. Toss to coat the ingredients evenly.
2. Preheat your air fryer to 375°F (190°C).
3. Place the marinated steak and vegetables in the air fryer basket.
4. Air fry at 375°F (190°C) for about 12-15 minutes, stirring once or twice, until the steak is cooked to your desired level of doneness and the vegetables are tender.

5. While the fajitas are cooking, warm the tortillas in the microwave or on a hot skillet.
6. Spoon the cooked steak and vegetables onto the warmed tortillas.
7. Serve with sour cream, guacamole, and salsa.

Air Fryer Duck Breast with Port Wine Reduction

Serves 2 / Prep Time: 10 minutes / Cook Time: 20 minutes

- 2 duck breast fillets (about 200g each)
- Salt and pepper, to taste
- 50ml port wine
- 10g unsalted butter
- 10g shallots, finely chopped
- 5g fresh thyme leaves
- 5g fresh rosemary leaves
- 10g sugar

1. Preheat your Ninja Foodi Dual Zone Air Fryer to 375°F (190°C) on the "Air Fry" setting.
2. Score the skin of the duck breasts with a crosshatch pattern, being careful not to cut into the meat.
3. Season the duck breasts with salt and pepper.
4. In one air fryer zone, place the seasoned duck breasts skin-side down.
5. Air fry at 375°F (190°C) for about 10 minutes.
6. In the other air fryer zone, melt unsalted butter and sauté chopped shallots until they become translucent. Add fresh thyme and rosemary leaves and cook for a minute.
7. Pour in port wine and sugar. Cook for another 5-7 minutes, allowing the mixture to reduce and thicken into a sauce.
8. After the duck breasts have cooked for 10 minutes, flip them over and air fry for an additional 7-10 minutes, depending on how well-done you prefer your duck.
9. Serve the duck breasts with the port wine reduction sauce drizzled over them.
10. Enjoy your Air Fryer Duck Breast with Port Wine Reduction!

Air Fryer Greek Potatoes

Serves 2 / Prep Time: 15 minutes / Cook Time: 30 minutes

- 400g baby potatoes, quartered
- 10g olive oil
- 5g dried oregano
- 5g garlic powder
- 5g onion powder
- Salt and black pepper to taste
- Cooking spray

1. In a bowl, toss the quartered baby potatoes with olive oil, dried oregano, garlic powder, onion powder, salt, and black pepper until well coated.
2. Preheat your Ninja Foodi Dual Zone Air Fryer to 375°F (190°C).
3. Spray the air fryer basket with cooking spray and place the seasoned potatoes inside.
4. Air fry at 375°F (190°C) for 25-30 minutes, shaking the basket halfway through, until the potatoes are crispy and cooked through.

Air Fryer Beef and Mushroom Duxelles Crepes

Serves 2 / Prep Time: 20 minutes / Cook Time: 15 minutes

- For the Crepes:
- 100g all-purpose flour
- 2 eggs
- 250ml milk
- Salt and pepper, to taste
- 10g unsalted butter, melted
- For the Filling:
- 200g beef tenderloin, thinly sliced
- 150g mushrooms, finely chopped
- 10g shallots, finely chopped
- 10g garlic, minced
- 10g fresh thyme leaves
- 20ml red wine
- 10g unsalted butter
- Salt and pepper, to taste

1. Preheat your Ninja Foodi Dual Zone Air Fryer to 375°F (190°C) on the "Bake/Roast" setting.
2. Prepare the crepe batter by whisking together flour, eggs, milk, melted butter, salt, and pepper until smooth. Let it rest for 10 minutes.
3. Pour a ladleful of the crepe batter into a hot, lightly greased pan. Swirl to coat the pan evenly and cook for about 1-2 minutes on each side until they are lightly golden. Make 4 crepes and set them aside.
4. In one air fryer zone, place the beef slices.
5. Air fry at 375°F (190°C) for about 5-7 minutes or until they are cooked to your desired level of doneness. Remove and set aside.
6. In the other air fryer zone, melt unsalted butter and sauté shallots and garlic until they become translucent.
7. Add the chopped mushrooms and fresh thyme leaves, and sauté for a few minutes.

8. Pour in the red wine and continue to cook until it reduces.
9. Add the cooked beef to the mushroom mixture and stir. Season with salt and pepper.
10. Lay out the crepes and spoon the beef and mushroom duxelles mixture onto each one.
11. Roll the crepes up, tucking in the sides as you go.
12. Place them back in the air fryer for a few minutes to warm.
13. Serve your Air Fryer Beef and Mushroom Duxelles Crepes hot.

Air Fryer Mac and Cheese

Serves 2 / Prep Time: 10 minutes / Cook Time: 15 minutes

- 150g elbow macaroni
- 150g shredded cheddar cheese
- 50g shredded mozzarella cheese
- 50g cream cheese
- 150ml milk
- 1/4 tsp garlic powder
- 1/4 tsp onion powder
- Salt and pepper to taste
- 30g breadcrumbs
- Cooking spray

1. Cook the macaroni according to package instructions until al dente. Drain and set aside.
2. In a saucepan, combine the cheddar cheese, mozzarella cheese, cream cheese, milk, garlic powder, onion powder, salt, and pepper. Cook over low heat, stirring until the cheeses are melted and the sauce is smooth.
3. Mix the cooked macaroni into the cheese sauce until well coated.
4. Preheat your Ninja Foodi Dual Zone Air Fryer to 350°F (175°C).
5. In a separate bowl, combine breadcrumbs and a little cooking spray to moisten them.
6. Fill the air fryer basket with the mac and cheese mixture.
7. Sprinkle the breadcrumb mixture evenly on top of the mac and cheese.
8. Air fry at 350°F (175°C) for 12-15 minutes until the top is golden brown and the mac and cheese is hot and bubbly.

Air Fryer Gourmet Pizza

Serves 2 / Prep Time: 15 minutes / Cook Time: 10 minutes

- 2 pre-made pizza dough rounds (150g each)
- 100g pizza sauce
- 150g mozzarella cheese, shredded
- 50g pepperoni slices
- 50g sliced black olives
- 50g sliced bell peppers
- 50g sliced mushrooms
- 5g dried oregano
- 5g dried basil
- Olive oil (for brushing)
- Salt and pepper, to taste

1. Preheat your Ninja Foodi Dual Zone Air Fryer to 375°F (190°C) on the "Air Fry" setting.
2. Roll out the pizza dough rounds into your desired thickness.
3. Brush olive oil on both sides of the pizza dough rounds.
4. Spread pizza sauce evenly over each dough.
5. In one air fryer zone, place one of the prepared pizza dough rounds.
6. Air fry at 375°F (190°C) for about 3-4 minutes or until the crust starts to become golden.
7. In the other air fryer zone, place the second prepared pizza dough round.
8. Air fry at 375°F (190°C) for about 3-4 minutes as well.
9. After air frying the crusts, remove them from the air fryer.
10. Top the crusts with mozzarella cheese, pepperoni, olives, bell peppers, and mushrooms.
11. Season with dried oregano, dried basil, salt, and pepper.
12. Return the pizzas to the air fryer and cook for an additional 4-6 minutes or until the cheese is bubbly and slightly browned.
13. Serve your Air Fryer Gourmet Pizza hot.

Steak and Kidney Pie

Serves: 4-6 / Prep time: 20 minutes / Cook time: 35-40 minutes

- 500 g beef steak, diced
- 226 g beef kidney, diced
- 1 large onion, chopped
- 2 cloves garlic, minced
- 2 tbsp. all-purpose flour
- 104 g of beef broth
- 1 tbsp. Worcestershire sauce
- 1 tbsp. tomato paste
- 1 tbsp. fresh thyme leaves chopped
- 1 tbsp. fresh rosemary leaves chopped
- Salt and pepper to taste
- 1 sheet of puff pastry, thawed
- 1 egg, beaten

1. Preheat the Ninja Dual Zone to 190°C in Bake mode.
2. In a large bowl, combine the diced beef steak and kidney with the chopped onion, minced garlic, and flour. Toss to coat well.
3. In a separate bowl, whisk together the beef broth, Worcestershire sauce, tomato paste, chopped thyme and rosemary, and salt and pepper to taste.
4. Pour the broth mixture over the beef and kidney mixture and stir to combine.
5. Transfer the mixture to a deep baking dish or pie dish.
6. Roll out the puff pastry sheet on a floured surface to fit the top of the dish. Cut a few slits in the top to allow steam to escape.
7. Brush the beaten egg over the top of the puff pastry.
8. Bake in the Ninja Dual Zone for 35-40 minutes, or until the pastry is golden brown and the filling is hot and bubbly.
9. Let cool for a few minutes before serving.

Roast Chicken with Vegetables

Serves: 4-6 / Prep time: 10 minutes / Cook time: 1 hour 15 minutes

- 1 whole chicken, about 4-5 pounds
- 4-5 medium potatoes, cut into 1-inch pieces
- 3-4 large carrots, peeled and cut into 1-inch pieces
- 1 onion, cut into wedges
- 2-3 cloves of garlic, minced
- 1 tablespoon olive oil
- 1 teaspoon salt
- 1/2 teaspoon black pepper
- 1 teaspoon paprika
- 1/2 teaspoon dried thyme
- 1/2 teaspoon dried rosemary

1. Preheat the Ninja Dual Zone to Roast mode at 190°C.
2. In a large bowl, combine the potatoes, carrots, onion, garlic, olive oil, salt, pepper, paprika, thyme, and rosemary. Toss to coat the vegetables evenly with the spices and oil.
3. Pat the chicken dry with paper towels, then season the inside and outside of the chicken generously with salt and pepper.
4. Stuff the chicken cavity with some of the vegetable mixtures, reserving the rest for later.
5. Place the chicken on the Ninja Dual Zone's cooking tray or a roasting pan.
6. Arrange the remaining vegetable mixture around the chicken in the cooking tray or roasting pan.
7. Roast the chicken and vegetables in the Ninja Dual Zone for 1 hour and 15 minutes, or until the chicken is cooked through and the vegetables are tender and caramelized.
8. Let the chicken rest for 10-15 minutes before carving and serving with the roasted vegetables.

Beef and Ale Stew

Serves: 4-6 / Prep time: 20 minutes / Cook time: 2 hours 15 minutes

- 1000 g beef stew meat, cut into 1-inch cubes
- 2 tbsp all-purpose flour
- Salt and pepper
- 2 tbsp vegetable oil
- 1 onion, chopped
- 2 cloves garlic, minced
- 3 medium carrots, peeled and chopped
- 2 stalks of celery, chopped
- 256g of beef broth
- 128g ale
- 2 tbsp tomato paste
- 1 tsp dried thyme
- 1 bay leaf
- 128g frozen peas

1. Preheat the Ninja Dual Zone to the "Roast" mode at 190°C.
2. In a large bowl, season the beef with salt and pepper, then toss with flour to coat.
3. Heat the vegetable oil in a Dutch oven over medium-high heat. Add the beef in batches and cook until browned on all sides. Remove the beef and set aside.
4. Add the onion and garlic to the Dutch oven and cook until softened about 5 minutes.

5. Add the carrots and celery and cook for another 5 minutes.
6. Add the beef broth, ale, tomato paste, thyme, and bay leaf. Stir well to combine.
7. Return the beef to the Dutch oven and bring the mixture to a simmer.
8. Cover the Dutch oven with a lid and transfer it to the Ninja Dual Zone Ninja Dual . Cook for 2 hours at 190°C in "Roast" mode, or until the beef is tender.
9. Remove the lid from the Dutch oven and stir in the frozen peas. Cook for another 5-10 minutes until the peas are heated through.
10. Serve hot with your favourite crusty bread.

Spaghetti Bolognese

Serves: 4-6 / Prep time: 10 minutes / Cook time: 40 minutes

- 500 g ground beef
- 1 onion, finely chopped
- 3 cloves garlic, minced
- 1 red bell pepper, chopped
- 226 g crushed tomatoes
- 1 teaspoon dried basil
- 1 teaspoon dried oregano
- 1 teaspoon salt
- 1/2 teaspoon black pepper
- 1/4 teaspoon red pepper flakes
- 1 tablespoon olive oil
- 500 g spaghetti
- Grated Parmesan cheese, for serving

1. Preheat the Ninja Dual Zone to sauté mode.
2. Add the olive oil to the inner pot and sauté the onion, garlic and red bell pepper until the onion is translucent about 5 minutes.
3. Add the ground beef to the inner pot and cook, breaking it up with a spatula, until browned about 10 minutes.
4. Add the crushed tomatoes, basil, oregano, salt, black pepper and red pepper flakes to the inner pot and stir to combine.
5. Close the lid and set the Ninja Dual Zone to pressure cook mode on high pressure for 15 minutes.
6. Once the cooking is complete, release the pressure manually and open the lid.
7. Meanwhile, cook the spaghetti according to the package Preparation Instructions.
8. Serve the Bolognese sauce over the cooked spaghetti and sprinkle with grated Parmesan cheese. Enjoy!

Thai Green Curry

Serves: 4-6 / Prep time: 15 minutes / Cook time: 15 minutes

- 1 tablespoon vegetable oil
- 2 tablespoons green curry paste
- 500 g of boneless, skinless chicken breasts or thighs, cut into bite-sized pieces
- 400 ml coconut milk
- 128g chicken broth
- 1 red bell pepper, sliced
- 1 green bell pepper, sliced
- 1 onion, sliced
- 2 teaspoons fish sauce
- 1 teaspoon brown sugar
- 1 lime, juiced
- 32g chopped fresh cilantro
- Cooked rice, for serving

1. Set the Ninja Dual Zone to Air Fry mode and preheat to 200°C.
2. Heat the vegetable oil in a large skillet over medium heat. Add the green curry paste and cook for 1-2 minutes until fragrant.
3. Add the chicken to the skillet and cook until browned on all sides, about 5 minutes.
4. Add the coconut milk, chicken broth, bell peppers, onion, fish sauce, and brown sugar to the skillet. Stir to combine.
5. Pour the mixture into the Ninja Dual Zone basket and cook for 10-15 minutes until the chicken is cooked through and the vegetables are tender.
6. Stir in the lime juice and cilantro. Serve over cooked rice.

Chapter 4 Beef, Pork and Lamb

Air Fryer Pork Belly

Serves 2 / Prep Time: 15 minutes / Cook Time: 30 minutes

- 300g pork belly, sliced into 1-inch strips
- 10g soy sauce
- 10g hoisin sauce
- 5g minced garlic
- 5g minced ginger
- 5g brown sugar
- 5g five-spice powder
- Cooking spray

1. In a bowl, mix soy sauce, hoisin sauce, minced garlic, minced ginger, brown sugar, and five-spice powder.
2. Toss the pork belly strips in the marinade and let them sit for 15 minutes.
3. Preheat your Ninja Foodi Dual Zone Air Fryer to 375°F (190°C).
4. Spray the air fryer basket with cooking spray and place the marinated pork belly strips inside, ensuring they are not touching.
5. Air fry at 375°F (190°C) for 25-30 minutes, flipping the pork belly strips halfway through, until they are crispy and cooked through.

Air Fryer Beef Wellington with Foie Gras

Serves 2 / Prep Time: 30 minutes / Cook Time: 25 minutes

- 2 beef tenderloin steaks (about 150g each)
- Salt and pepper, to taste
- 100g foie gras
- 2 sheets of puff pastry dough
- 10g Dijon mustard
- 10g olive oil
- 1 egg (beaten, for egg wash)

1. Preheat your Ninja Foodi Dual Zone Air Fryer to 375°F (190°C) on the "Bake/Roast" setting.
2. Season the beef tenderloin steaks with salt and pepper.
3. In a pan, sear the steaks on high heat with olive oil for about 1-2 minutes on each side to get a nice crust.
4. In one air fryer zone, place the foie gras and air fry at 375°F (190°C) for about 5 minutes, or until it's heated through.
5. In the other air fryer zone, cut the puff pastry sheets into rectangles large enough to wrap the beef and foie gras.
6. Place one steak on each piece of puff pastry.
7. Top the steaks with foie gras.
8. Brush Dijon mustard over the foie gras.
9. Wrap the puff pastry around the steaks and foie gras, sealing the edges.
10. Brush the pastry with egg wash for a golden finish.
11. Air fry the Beef Wellingtons at 375°F (190°C) for about 15-20 minutes, or until the pastry is golden and the beef is cooked to your desired level of doneness.
12. Serve your Air Fryer Beef Wellington with Foie Gras.

Air Fryer Beef Rouladen

Serves 2 / Prep Time: 20 minutes / Cook Time: 25 minute

- For the Beef Rouladen:
- 300g beef round or sirloin steak, thinly sliced
- 30g Dijon mustard
- 60g bacon, diced
- 60g onion, finely chopped
- 60g dill pickles, sliced into thin strips
- Salt and black pepper to taste
- 20g vegetable oil
- For the Gravy:
- 20g all-purpose flour
- 200ml beef broth
- 30ml red wine
- 5g fresh parsley, chopped

1. Preheat your Ninja Foodi Dual Zone Air Fryer to 375°F (190°C) on the "Air Fry" setting.
2. Pound the beef slices to an even thickness, then spread Dijon mustard over them.
3. In a skillet, cook the diced bacon until it's crisp, then remove it and set aside.
4. In the same skillet, sauté the finely chopped onion until it's translucent.
5. Place a slice of beef on a work surface, and add a strip of bacon, some sautéed onions, and a strip of dill pickle. Season with salt and black pepper.
6. Roll up the beef, securing it with toothpicks.
7. Repeat the process for all beef slices.
8. Place the beef rouladen in one air fryer zone.

9. Air fry at 375°F (190°C) for about 20-25 minutes, turning them occasionally, until they are browned and cooked through.
10. In the other air fryer zone, mix all-purpose flour with beef broth and red wine to create the gravy.
11. Air fry the gravy mixture at 375°F (190°C) for about 5 minutes, or until it thickens.
12. Serve the beef rouladen with the gravy and garnish with fresh parsley.
13. Enjoy your Air Fryer Beef Rouladen!

Air Fryer Stuffed Flank Steak

Serves 2 / Prep Time: 20 minutes / Cook Time: 20 minutes

- 2 flank steak slices (about 250g each)
- 100g spinach leaves
- 100g feta cheese, crumbled
- 50g sun-dried tomatoes, chopped
- 5g garlic powder
- 5g onion powder
- Salt and black pepper to taste
- Kitchen twine for tying

1. Preheat your Ninja Foodi Dual Zone Air Fryer to 375°F (190°C) on the "Air Fry" setting.
2. Lay the flank steak slices flat and season with garlic powder, onion powder, salt, and black pepper.
3. On each flank steak slice, layer spinach leaves, crumbled feta cheese, and chopped sun-dried tomatoes.
4. Roll up the flank steak slices, securing the filling with kitchen twine.
5. Place the stuffed flank steaks in the air fryer basket.
6. Air fry at 375°F (190°C) for about 18-20 minutes, or until the steak reaches your desired level of doneness (medium-rare at 130°F/54°C, medium at 140°F/60°C).
7. Remove from the air fryer, let them rest for a few minutes, and then slice.
8. Serve your Stuffed Flank Steak hot and enjoy.

Air Fryer Parmesan-Crusted Rack of Lamb

Serves 2 / Prep Time: 15 minutes / Cook Time: 20 minutes

- 1 rack of lamb (about 400g)
- 30g Dijon mustard
- 50g breadcrumbs
- 30g grated Parmesan cheese
- 5g dried rosemary
- 10g olive oil
- Salt and black pepper to taste

1. Preheat your Ninja Foodi Dual Zone Air Fryer to 400°F (200°C) on the "Air Fry" setting.
2. Season the rack of lamb with salt and black pepper.
3. In a bowl, mix the Dijon mustard, breadcrumbs, grated Parmesan cheese, dried rosemary, and olive oil to create the crust mixture.
4. Press the crust mixture onto the rack of lamb.
5. Place the rack of lamb in the air fryer basket.
6. Air fry at 400°F (200°C) for about 18-20 minutes, or until the lamb reaches your desired level of doneness (130°F/54°C for medium-rare, 140°F/60°C for medium).
7. Remove from the air fryer, let it rest for a few minutes, then slice into chops.
8. Serve your Parmesan-Crusted Rack of Lamb hot.
9. Enjoy this gourmet dish!

Air Fryer Beef and Black Bean Stir-Fry

Serves 2 / Prep Time: 20 minutes / Cook Time: 15 minutes

- 300g flank steak, thinly sliced
- 100g black bean sauce
- 100g green bell pepper, sliced
- 100g red bell pepper, sliced
- 100g broccoli florets
- 100g sliced carrots
- 2 cloves garlic, minced
- 10g ginger, minced
- 5g cornstarch
- 5g vegetable oil
- Salt and black pepper to taste
- Cooked rice or noodles (for serving)

1. Preheat your Ninja Foodi Dual Zone Air Fryer to 400°F (200°C) on the "Air Fry" setting.
2. In a bowl, mix the sliced flank steak with salt, black pepper, and cornstarch until the meat is coated.
3. In a separate bowl, combine the black bean sauce, minced garlic, and minced ginger.
4. Place the sliced flank steak in one of the air fryer zones.
5. Air fry at 400°F (200°C) for about 6-8 minutes, or until the beef is browned and cooked through.
6. In the other zone, add the vegetable oil and the sliced vegetables. Air fry at 400°F (200°C) for about 8-10 minutes, or until they are tender and slightly crispy.
7. Return the cooked beef to the vegetables and pour the black bean sauce mixture over everything.
8. Air fry for an additional 2-3 minutes until the sauce is heated through.
9. Serve your Beef and Black Bean Stir-Fry over

cooked rice or noodles, and enjoy.

Air Fryer Pork Belly Bao Buns

Serves 2 / Prep Time: 20 minutes / Cook Time: 30 minutes

- 200g pork belly slices
- 4 bao buns
- 20g hoisin sauce
- 20g soy sauce
- 10g sesame oil
- 10g rice vinegar
- 5g brown sugar
- 5g fresh ginger, minced
- 5g garlic, minced
- Sliced cucumbers, green onions, and fresh cilantro for garnish

1. Preheat your Ninja Foodi Dual Zone Air Fryer to 375°F (190°C) on the "Air Fry" setting.
2. In a bowl, mix hoisin sauce, soy sauce, sesame oil, rice vinegar, brown sugar, minced ginger, and minced garlic to create a marinade for the pork belly.
3. Marinate the pork belly slices in this mixture for about 15 minutes.
4. In one air fryer zone, place the marinated pork belly slices.
5. Air fry at 375°F (190°C) for about 15-20 minutes, turning them halfway through, until they are crispy and cooked.
6. In the other zone, warm the bao buns for about 3-5 minutes.
7. Assemble the bao buns by placing a slice of pork belly in each bun, garnishing with sliced cucumbers, green onions, and fresh cilantro.
8. Serve your Pork Belly Bao Buns with the garnishes and extra sauce for dipping.
9. Enjoy this delicious Asian-inspired dish!

Air Fryer Beef Stir-Fry

Serves 2 / Prep Time: 15 minutes / Cook Time: 15 minutes

- 200g beef sirloin, thinly sliced
- 100g broccoli florets
- 100g bell peppers, sliced
- 100g snow peas
- 5g garlic, minced
- 5g ginger, minced
- 30g soy sauce
- 10g oyster sauce
- 10g cornstarch
- 5g vegetable oil
- 5g sesame oil
- Salt and black pepper to taste

1. Preheat your Ninja Foodi Dual Zone Air Fryer to 375°F (190°C) on the "Air Fry" setting.
2. In a bowl, combine the thinly sliced beef, minced garlic, minced ginger, soy sauce, oyster sauce, cornstarch, vegetable oil, and sesame oil. Toss to coat the beef and let it marinate for about 10 minutes.
3. In one air fryer zone, arrange the marinated beef slices in a single layer.
4. In the other zone, arrange the broccoli florets, bell peppers, and snow peas.
5. Air fry at 375°F (190°C) for about 12-15 minutes, tossing the vegetables and stirring the beef once or twice during cooking, until the beef is cooked and the vegetables are tender-crisp.
6. Serve your Beef Stir-Fry hot over steamed rice or noodles.
7. Enjoy this savory and quick meal!

Air Fryer Beef Tournedos Rossini

Serves 2 / Prep Time: 15 minutes / Cook Time: 20 minutes

- 2 beef tournedos (filet mignon) steaks (about 200g each)
- 50g foie gras (goose or duck liver)
- 10g black truffle, thinly sliced (optional)
- 50g beef demi-glace sauce
- 30g butter
- Salt and black pepper to taste

1. Preheat your Ninja Foodi Dual Zone Air Fryer to 375°F (190°C) on the "Roast" setting.
2. Season the beef tournedos with salt and black pepper.
3. In a skillet, sear the foie gras for about 2 minutes on each side or until golden brown.
4. Place the seasoned beef tournedos in one of the air fryer zones.
5. Air fry at 375°F (190°C) for about 10-15 minutes, turning them halfway through, until they reach your desired level of doneness (120°F/49°C for rare, 130°F/54°C for medium-rare, 140°F/60°C for medium).
6. Once done, remove the beef tournedos from the air fryer.
7. In the other zone, warm the demi-glace sauce.
8. Top each beef tournedo with foie gras, truffle slices (if using), and a drizzle of the warmed demi-glace sauce.
9. Serve your Beef Tournedos Rossini hot and enjoy

this luxurious dish.

Air Fryer Italian Meatballs

Serves 2 / Prep Time: 15 minutes / Cook Time: 15 minutes

- 200g ground beef
- 10g bread crumbs
- 10g grated Parmesan cheese
- 5g Italian seasoning
- 5g minced garlic
- 5g chopped fresh parsley
- 1 egg
- Salt and black pepper to taste

1. In a mixing bowl, combine the ground beef, bread crumbs, grated Parmesan cheese, Italian seasoning, minced garlic, chopped fresh parsley, egg, salt, and black pepper. Mix until all ingredients are well combined.
2. Shape the mixture into 6 meatballs, each about 1.5 inches in diameter.
3. Preheat your Ninja Foodi Dual Zone Air Fryer to 375°F (190°C) on the "Air Fry" setting.
4. Place the meatballs in the air fryer basket, ensuring they are spaced apart.
5. Air fry at 375°F (190°C) for about 15 minutes, turning the meatballs over halfway through the cooking time, until they are browned and cooked through.
6. Once done, remove the meatballs from the air fryer.
7. Serve the Italian meatballs with your choice of sauce or pasta, and enjoy.

Air Fryer Beef Tenderloin with Gorgonzola Sauce

Serves 2 / Prep Time: 15 minutes / Cook Time: 15 minutes

- 2 beef tenderloin steaks (about 200g each)
- 50g Gorgonzola cheese, crumbled
- 30g heavy cream
- 10g butter
- Salt and black pepper to taste

1. Preheat your Ninja Foodi Dual Zone Air Fryer to 400°F (200°C) on the "Roast" setting.
2. Season the beef tenderloin steaks with salt and black pepper.
3. In a small saucepan, melt the butter over low heat. Add the Gorgonzola cheese and heavy cream. Stir until the cheese is melted and the sauce is smooth. Keep warm.
4. Place the seasoned beef tenderloin steaks in the air fryer basket.
5. Air fry at 400°F (200°C) for about 15 minutes or until the desired level of doneness is reached. Use a meat thermometer to check for your preferred level (120°F/49°C for rare, 130°F/54°C for medium-rare, 140°F/60°C for medium).
6. Serve the beef tenderloin steaks with the Gorgonzola sauce drizzled over the top.
7. Enjoy your Beef Tenderloin with Gorgonzola Sauce.

Air Fryer Beef and Blue Cheese-Stuffed Peppers

Serves 2 / Prep Time: 20 minutes / Cook Time: 15 minutes

- 2 large bell peppers
- 200g ground beef
- 50g blue cheese, crumbled
- 50g diced tomatoes
- 50g onions, chopped
- 2 cloves garlic, minced
- 5g olive oil
- 5g Italian seasoning
- Salt and black pepper to taste

1. Cut the tops off the bell peppers and remove the seeds and membranes.
2. In a bowl, mix the ground beef, blue cheese, diced tomatoes, chopped onions, minced garlic, Italian seasoning, salt, and black pepper.
3. Preheat your Ninja Foodi Dual Zone Air Fryer to 375°F (190°C) on the "Air Fry" setting.
4. In one of the air fryer zones, heat the olive oil using the "Sear/Sauté" function. Add the beef mixture and cook until the meat is browned and cooked through.
5. Stuff the hollowed bell peppers with the beef and cheese mixture.
6. Place the stuffed peppers in the air fryer basket and air fry at 375°F (190°C) for 15 minutes, or until the peppers are tender.
7. Serve your Beef and Blue Cheese-Stuffed Peppers hot and enjoy.

Air Fryer Beef Wellington

Serves 2 / Prep Time: 30 minutes / Cook Time: 30 minutes

- 2 beef fillet steaks (about 200g each)
- 100g cremini mushrooms, chopped
- 10g olive oil
- 2 cloves garlic, minced
- 100g puff pastry

- 2 slices prosciutto
- 20g Dijon mustard
- Salt and black pepper to taste
- 1 egg (for egg wash)

1. Preheat your Ninja Foodi Dual Zone Air Fryer to 400°F (200°C) on the "Roast" setting.
2. Season the beef fillet steaks with salt and black pepper.
3. In a skillet, sauté the chopped cremini mushrooms with olive oil and minced garlic until they release their moisture and become dry.
4. In one of the air fryer zones, sear the seasoned beef fillet steaks on high heat for about 2 minutes on each side. Remove and let them cool.
5. On a lightly floured surface, roll out the puff pastry into two rectangles.
6. Spread Dijon mustard on each piece of prosciutto and wrap it around the beef fillet steaks.
7. Place the prosciutto-wrapped fillets on the puff pastry rectangles.
8. Wrap the puff pastry around the fillets and brush with beaten egg for an egg wash.
9. Place the wrapped Beef Wellingtons in the air fryer and air fry at 400°F (200°C) for about 20-25 minutes, or until the pastry is golden brown and the beef is cooked to your desired level (120°F/49°C for rare, 130°F/54°C for medium-rare).
10. Serve your Beef Wellington hot, and enjoy this elegant dish.

Air Fryer Herb-Crusted Lamb Chops

Serves 2 / Prep Time: 15 minutes / Cook Time: 12 minutes

- 4 lamb chops (about 150g each)
- 10g fresh rosemary, chopped
- 10g fresh thyme, chopped
- 10g fresh parsley, chopped
- 10g breadcrumbs
- 10g Dijon mustard
- 20g olive oil
- Salt and pepper, to taste

1. Preheat your Ninja Foodi Dual Zone Air Fryer to 375°F (190°C) on the "Air Fry" setting.
2. Season the lamb chops with salt and pepper.
3. In a bowl, combine chopped fresh rosemary, thyme, parsley, breadcrumbs, Dijon mustard, and olive oil to create a herb crust.
4. In one air fryer zone, place the seasoned lamb chops.
5. In the other air fryer zone, spread the herb crust mixture evenly on a tray.
6. Air fry the lamb chops at 375°F (190°C) for about 6 minutes on each side, or until they reach your desired level of doneness.
7. Simultaneously, air fry the herb crust mixture for about 5 minutes until it becomes crispy.
8. Serve the lamb chops with the herb crust mixture on top.
9. Enjoy your Air Fryer Herb-Crusted Lamb Chops!

Italian Prosciutto-Wrapped Beef Tenderloin

Serves: 4 / Prep time: 15 minutes / Cook time: 20 minutes

- 4 beef tenderloin fillets, about 150g each
- 8 thin slices of prosciutto
- 1 tbsp olive oil
- Salt and black pepper, to taste
- 2 tbsp butter
- 2 cloves garlic, minced
- 2 sprigs of fresh thyme
- 120ml beef broth

1. Preheat the Ninja Dual Zone Air Fryer to 200°C on zone 1 for 5 minutes.
2. Wrap each beef tenderloin fillet with 2 slices of prosciutto, making sure the prosciutto covers the entire fillet.
3. Brush the fillets with olive oil and season with salt and black pepper.
4. Place the fillets on the crisper plate in zone 1 of the air fryer and air fry for 10 minutes.
5. While the fillets are cooking, prepare the sauce by melting the butter in a small saucepan over medium heat. Add the garlic and cook for 1 minute.
6. Add the thyme and beef broth to the saucepan and bring to a simmer. Cook for 5 minutes or until the sauce has thickened.
7. Once the fillets are cooked, remove them from the air fryer and let them rest for a few minutes. Serve with the sauce on top.

Mexican Chorizo Stuffed Jalapeño Poppers

Serves: 4 / Prep time: 10 minutes / Cook time: 15 minutes

- 8 large jalapeño peppers
- 1/2 lb chorizo sausage, removed from casing
- 4 oz cream cheese, softened
- 60g grated cheddar cheese
- Salt and black pepper, to taste

1. Preheat the Ninja Dual Zone Air Fryer to 190°C on zone 1 for 5 minutes.
2. Cut off the stem end of each jalapeño pepper, then slice each pepper in half lengthwise and remove the seeds and membranes.
3. In a skillet over medium heat, cook the chorizo sausage until browned and cooked through, breaking it up into small pieces with a wooden spoon.
4. In a mixing bowl, combine the cooked chorizo, cream cheese, cheddar cheese, salt, and black pepper.
5. Stuff each jalapeño half with the chorizo mixture, filling each one evenly.
6. Place the stuffed jalapeño halves on the crisper plate in zone 1 and air fry at 190°C for 10-15 minutes, until the jalapeños are tender and the filling is golden brown and crispy.
7. Once cooked, remove from the air fryer and serve immediately.

Spicy Korean Pork Belly

Serves: 2 / Prep time: 10 minutes / Cook time: 30 minutes

- 400g pork belly slices
- 1 tbsp gochujang (Korean chilli paste)
- 2 tbsp soy sauce
- 2 tbsp honey
- 1 tbsp rice vinegar
- 1 tbsp sesame oil
- 1 tbsp minced garlic
- 1 tbsp minced ginger
- 2 green onions, thinly sliced
- 1 tbsp toasted sesame seeds

1. In a bowl, mix together the gochujang, soy sauce, honey, rice vinegar, sesame oil, garlic, and ginger.
2. Add the pork belly slices to the bowl and toss to coat evenly.
3. Let the pork belly marinate for at least 10 minutes, or up to overnight in the fridge.
4. Preheat the Ninja Dual Zone Air Fryer in "AIRFRYER" mode to 200°C for 5 minutes.
5. Place the pork belly slices on the crisper plate in zone 2 and cook for 15 minutes.
6. After 15 minutes, flip the pork belly slices and cook for another 10-15 minutes until the pork is crispy and fully cooked.
7. Serve with sliced green onions and toasted sesame seeds.

Vietnamese Grilled Lemongrass Pork Chops

Serves: 2 / Prep time: 10 minutes + 2 hours marinating time / Cook time: 10 minutes

- 2 pork chops
- 2 stalks lemongrass, finely chopped
- 3 garlic cloves, minced
- 1 tbsp fish sauce
- 1 tbsp soy sauce
- 1 tbsp brown sugar
- 1 tsp sesame oil
- 1/4 tsp black pepper
- 2 tbsp vegetable oil
- Lime wedges, for serving

1. In a small bowl, whisk together lemongrass, garlic, fish sauce, soy sauce, brown sugar, sesame oil, and black pepper.
2. Place pork chops in a shallow dish or ziplock bag, and pour the marinade over them. Turn to coat evenly. Marinate in the refrigerator for at least 2 hours, or overnight.
3. Heat vegetable oil in a grill pan or on a barbecue grill over high heat.
4. Remove pork chops from the marinade, and discard the excess marinade.
5. Grill pork chops for 3-4 minutes on each side, or until cooked through and nicely charred.
6. Serve hot and enjoy!

Chapter 5 Fish and Seafood

Air Fryer Asian Glazed Salmon

Serves 2 / Prep Time: 15 minutes / Cook Time: 15 minutes

- 2 salmon fillets (180g each)
- 2 tablespoons soy sauce
- 1 tablespoon honey
- 1 tablespoon rice vinegar
- 1 teaspoon sesame oil
- 1/2 teaspoon grated ginger
- 1/2 teaspoon minced garlic
- 1/2 teaspoon red pepper flakes (adjust to your spice preference)
- 2 green onions, chopped
- Sesame seeds for garnish

1. In a small bowl, whisk together the soy sauce, honey, rice vinegar, sesame oil, grated ginger, minced garlic, and red pepper flakes to create the Asian glaze.
2. Preheat your Ninja Foodi Dual Zone Air Fryer to 375°F (190°C).
3. Place the salmon fillets in a shallow dish and brush them with the Asian glaze. Let them marinate for about 10 minutes.
4. Once the air fryer is preheated, place the salmon fillets in the air fryer basket.
5. Cook the salmon at 375°F (190°C) for about 12-15 minutes, depending on the thickness of the fillets. Check for doneness by ensuring the salmon flakes easily with a fork.
6. While the salmon is cooking, brush it with more glaze a couple of times during the cooking process to build up the flavor.
7. Once the salmon is cooked, remove it from the air fryer and garnish with chopped green onions and sesame seeds.

Air Fryer Crab-Stuffed Shrimp

Serves 2 / Prep Time: 20 minutes / Cook Time: 15 minutes

- For the Crab-Stuffed Shrimp:
- 12 large shrimp, peeled and deveined (about 300g)
- 100g lump crabmeat
- 1/4 cup mayonnaise
- 1/4 cup breadcrumbs
- 1 green onion, finely chopped
- 1/2 teaspoon Old Bay seasoning
- Salt and pepper to taste
- Lemon wedges for serving

1. In a bowl, combine lump crabmeat, mayonnaise, breadcrumbs, chopped green onion, Old Bay seasoning, salt, and pepper. Mix well to form the crab stuffing.
2. Take each shrimp and make a deep slit along the back, being careful not to cut all the way through.
3. Stuff each shrimp with a spoonful of the crab mixture.
4. Preheat your air fryer to 375°F (190°C).
5. Place the stuffed shrimp in the air fryer basket.
6. Air fry at 375°F (190°C) for about 12-15 minutes until the shrimp are pink, opaque, and the stuffing is heated through.

Fried Shrimp Po' Boy

Serves 2 / Prep Time: 20 minutes / Cook Time: 15 minutes

- For the Fried Shrimp:
- 200g large shrimp, peeled and deveined
- 100g all-purpose flour
- 5g paprika
- 5g garlic powder
- 5g salt
- 5g black pepper
- 1 egg
- Cooking oil, for frying
- For the Po' Boy Assembly:
- 2 small sub rolls or baguettes
- 60g shredded lettuce
- 60g sliced tomatoes
- 30g mayonnaise
- 20g hot sauce (adjust to taste)
- Lemon wedges

1. In a bowl, combine the all-purpose flour, paprika, garlic powder, salt, and black pepper for the shrimp coating.
2. In another bowl, beat the egg. Dip each shrimp into the egg, then into the flour mixture, ensuring they are well-coated.
3. Preheat your Ninja Foodi Dual Zone Air Fryer to 375°F (190°C) using the "Air Fry" setting.
4. Lightly grease the air fryer basket with cooking oil.
5. Place the coated shrimp in the air fryer basket.
6. Air fry for about 8-10 minutes or until the shrimp are golden and crispy.

7. While the shrimp is cooking, prepare the Po' Boy rolls by spreading mayonnaise and hot sauce on each roll. Layer with shredded lettuce, sliced tomatoes, and the fried shrimp.
8. Serve with lemon wedges.

Parmesan Crusted Fish

Serves 2 / Prep Time: 15 minutes / Cook Time: 15 minutes

- 300g white fish fillets (such as cod or tilapia)
- 30g grated Parmesan cheese
- 30g breadcrumbs
- 5g garlic powder
- 5g onion powder
- 5g salt
- 5g black pepper
- 1 egg
- Cooking oil, for brushing

1. Preheat your Ninja Foodi Dual Zone Air Fryer to 375°F (190°C) using the "Air Fry" setting.
2. In a bowl, combine grated Parmesan cheese, breadcrumbs, garlic powder, onion powder, salt, and black pepper.
3. In another bowl, beat the egg.
4. Dip each fish fillet into the egg, then coat it with the Parmesan and breadcrumb mixture, pressing the mixture onto the fish to adhere.
5. Lightly brush the air fryer basket with cooking oil.
6. Place the coated fish fillets in the air fryer basket.
7. Air fry for about 12-15 minutes or until the fish is cooked through and the coating is golden and crispy.

Air Fryer Cajun Shrimp and Sausage Foil Packets

Serves 2 / Prep Time: 20 minutes / Cook Time: 15 minutes

- 200g large shrimp, peeled and deveined
- 200g smoked sausage, sliced
- 150g bell peppers, diced
- 150g red onion, diced
- 10g Cajun seasoning
- 5g garlic powder
- 5g paprika
- Salt and black pepper to taste
- Cooking spray
- 2 sheets of aluminum foil

1. In a bowl, combine the shrimp, smoked sausage, bell peppers, red onion, Cajun seasoning, garlic powder, paprika, salt, and black pepper.
2. Place the mixture on the center of each aluminum foil sheet. Fold up the sides to create packets.
3. Preheat your Ninja Foodi Dual Zone Air Fryer to 375°F (190°C).
4. Spray the foil packets with cooking spray and place them in the air fryer basket.
5. Air fry at 375°F (190°C) for 12-15 minutes, or until the shrimp is cooked through and the veggies are tender.

Air Fryer Teriyaki Salmon

Serves 2 / Prep Time: 15 minutes / Cook Time: 12 minutes

- 2 salmon fillets (about 200g each)
- 50g teriyaki sauce
- 10g honey
- 5g minced ginger
- 5g minced garlic
- 5g sesame seeds
- Cooking spray

1. In a bowl, mix teriyaki sauce, honey, minced ginger, minced garlic, and sesame seeds to make the teriyaki marinade.
2. Marinate the salmon fillets in the teriyaki sauce mixture for 10 minutes.
3. Preheat your Ninja Foodi Dual Zone Air Fryer to 375°F (190°C).
4. Spray the air fryer basket with cooking spray and place the marinated salmon fillets inside.
5. Air fry at 375°F (190°C) for 10-12 minutes or until the salmon is cooked through and flakes easily with a fork.

Air Fryer Cilantro-Lime Shrimp

Serves 2 / Prep Time: 15 minutes / Cook Time: 8 minutes

- 300g large shrimp, peeled and deveined
- 10g olive oil
- Juice of 1 lime
- 10g fresh cilantro, chopped
- 5g minced garlic
- 5g chili powder
- Salt and black pepper to taste
- Cooking spray

1. In a bowl, mix the shrimp, olive oil, lime juice, chopped cilantro, minced garlic, chili powder, salt, and black pepper. Toss to coat the shrimp evenly.
2. Preheat your Ninja Foodi Dual Zone Air Fryer to 375°F (190°C).
3. Spray the air fryer basket with cooking spray and place the marinated shrimp inside.

4. Air fry at 375°F (190°C) for 8 minutes or until the shrimp turn pink and are cooked through.

Air Fryer Seafood Medley

Serves 2 / Prep Time: 15 minutes / Cook Time: 15 minutes

- For the Seafood Medley:
- 200g shrimp, peeled and deveined
- 200g scallops
- 200g mussels, cleaned and debearded
- 100g cherry tomatoes
- 100g bell peppers, diced
- 50g red onion, diced
- 5g garlic, minced
- 20g olive oil
- 5g lemon juice
- 5g fresh parsley, chopped
- Salt and black pepper to taste
- For the Lemon Garlic Butter Sauce:
- 20g butter
- 5g garlic, minced
- 5g lemon juice
- Salt and black pepper to taste

1. Preheat your Ninja Foodi Dual Zone Air Fryer to 375°F (190°C) on the "Air Fry" setting.
2. In a bowl, combine shrimp, scallops, mussels, cherry tomatoes, bell peppers, red onion, minced garlic, olive oil, lemon juice, fresh parsley, salt, and black pepper. Toss to coat.
3. In a small saucepan, melt the butter for the lemon garlic butter sauce. Add minced garlic, lemon juice, salt, and black pepper. Cook for a couple of minutes and set aside.
4. In one air fryer zone, place the prepared seafood medley.
5. Air fry at 375°F (190°C) for about 10-15 minutes, stirring occasionally, until the seafood is cooked, and the mussels have opened.
6. Drizzle the lemon garlic butter sauce over the seafood before serving.
7. Enjoy your Air Fryer Seafood Medley!

Air Fryer Crab Cakes

Serves 2 / Prep Time: 20 minutes / Cook Time: 15 minutes

- 200g lump crab meat
- 50g breadcrumbs
- 30g mayonnaise
- 10g Dijon mustard
- 5g Worcestershire sauce
- 5g Old Bay seasoning
- 5g minced parsley
- 1 egg, beaten
- Cooking spray

1. In a bowl, combine the crab meat, breadcrumbs, mayonnaise, Dijon mustard, Worcestershire sauce, Old Bay seasoning, minced parsley, and beaten egg.
2. Form the mixture into crab cakes and place them on a parchment-lined tray. Refrigerate for 10 minutes to firm up.
3. Preheat your Ninja Foodi Dual Zone Air Fryer to 375°F (190°C).
4. Spray the crab cakes with cooking spray and place them in the air fryer basket, ensuring they are not touching.
5. Air fry at 375°F (190°C) for 12-15 minutes, or until they are golden brown and cooked through.

Air Fryer Truffle-Crusted Scallops

Serves 2 / Prep Time: 15 minutes / Cook Time: 8 minutes

- 8 large sea scallops (about 150g each)
- 20g panko breadcrumbs
- 10g grated Parmesan cheese
- 5g black truffle oil
- 5g fresh parsley, chopped
- Salt and pepper, to taste
- Lemon wedges, for serving

1. Preheat your Ninja Foodi Dual Zone Air Fryer to 375°F (190°C) on the "Air Fry" setting.
2. Season the scallops with salt and pepper.
3. In a bowl, combine panko breadcrumbs, grated Parmesan cheese, chopped fresh parsley, and black truffle oil to form a crumbly mixture.
4. In one air fryer zone, place the seasoned scallops.
5. In the other air fryer zone, spread the truffle-crumb mixture evenly on a tray.
6. Air fry the scallops at 375°F (190°C) for about 4 minutes, then flip them and air fry for an additional 4 minutes, or until they are cooked through and the crust is golden brown.
7. Simultaneously, air fry the truffle-crumb mixture for about 5 minutes until it becomes golden and crispy.
8. Serve the truffle-crusted scallops on a plate with the crispy truffle crumb mixture.
9. Garnish with lemon wedges.
10. Enjoy your Air Fryer Truffle-Crusted Scallops!

Tempura-Battered Shrimp

Serves 2 / Prep Time: 15 minutes / Cook Time: 10 minutes

- 200g large shrimp, peeled and deveined
- 60g all-purpose flour
- 60g cornstarch
- 1/2 tsp salt
- 1/4 tsp black pepper
- 1/2 cup ice-cold sparkling water
- Cooking spray
- Dipping sauce (e. g. , soy sauce, tempura sauce)

1. In a mixing bowl, combine all-purpose flour, cornstarch, salt, and black pepper.
2. Gradually add ice-cold sparkling water and whisk until the batter is smooth. It should be quite thin.
3. Dip each shrimp into the batter, allowing any excess to drip off.
4. Preheat the Ninja Foodi Dual Zone Air Fryer to 400°F (200°C) using the "Air Fry" setting.
5. Place the battered shrimp in the Dual Zone Air Fryer basket, ensuring they are in a single layer and not overcrowded.
6. Spray the shrimp lightly with cooking spray.
7. Set the Dual Zone Air Fryer to Air Fry at 400°F (200°C) for 8-10 minutes or until the shrimp are golden brown and cooked through.
8. Serve hot with your preferred dipping sauce.

Air Fryer Salmon with Dill Cream Sauce

Serves 2 / Prep Time: 15 minutes / Cook Time: 12 minutes

- 2 salmon fillets (about 200g each)
- Salt and pepper, to taste
- 30ml olive oil
- 5g fresh dill, chopped
- 10ml lemon juice
- 60ml heavy cream
- 10g Dijon mustard

1. Preheat your Ninja Foodi Dual Zone Air Fryer to 375°F (190°C) on the "Air Fry" setting.
2. Season the salmon fillets with salt, pepper, and olive oil.
3. In a bowl, mix chopped fresh dill, lemon juice, heavy cream, and Dijon mustard to create the dill cream sauce.
4. In one air fryer zone, place the seasoned salmon fillets.
5. Air fry at 375°F (190°C) for about 10-12 minutes or until the salmon is cooked to your desired level of doneness.
6. In the other air fryer zone, heat the dill cream sauce for a few minutes until it's heated through.
7. Serve the Air Fryer Salmon with Dill Cream Sauce, drizzling the sauce over the fillets.

Air Fryer Lemon Herb Salmon Patties

Serves 2 / Prep Time: 15 minutes / Cook Time: 10 minutes

- For the Salmon Patties:
- 200g canned salmon, drained and flaked
- 50g breadcrumbs
- 1 egg
- 5g lemon zest
- 5g fresh dill, chopped
- 5g fresh parsley, chopped
- Salt and black pepper to taste
- 10g olive oil (for brushing)
- For the Lemon-Dill Sauce:
- 30g Greek yogurt
- 5g lemon juice
- 5g fresh dill, chopped
- Salt and black pepper to taste

1. Preheat your Ninja Foodi Dual Zone Air Fryer to 375°F (190°C) on the "Air Fry" setting.
2. In a bowl, combine the canned salmon, breadcrumbs, egg, lemon zest, fresh dill, fresh parsley, salt, and black pepper. Mix until well combined.
3. Form the mixture into two salmon patties.
4. In a separate bowl, prepare the lemon-dill sauce by combining Greek yogurt, lemon juice, fresh dill, salt, and black pepper.
5. Brush the salmon patties with olive oil.
6. Place the salmon patties in one air fryer zone.
7. Air fry at 375°F (190°C) for about 8-10 minutes, turning them halfway through, until they are golden and cooked through.
8. Serve the salmon patties with a dollop of lemon-dill sauce on top.
9. Enjoy your Air Fryer Lemon Herb Salmon Patties!

Air Fryer Shrimp Scampi

Serves 2 / Prep Time: 15 minutes / Cook Time: 10 minutes

- 200g large shrimp, peeled and deveined
- 100g linguine pasta
- 20g butter
- 20g olive oil
- 20g white wine
- 10g garlic, minced
- 10g fresh parsley, chopped
- 5g lemon juice
- Salt and black pepper to taste

- Red pepper flakes (optional for heat)

1. Preheat your Ninja Foodi Dual Zone Air Fryer to 375°F (190°C) on the "Air Fry" setting.
2. Cook the linguine pasta according to package instructions. Drain and set aside.
3. In a bowl, mix the shrimp, olive oil, white wine, minced garlic, chopped fresh parsley, lemon juice, salt, black pepper, and red pepper flakes if desired. Let the shrimp marinate for a few minutes.
4. In one of the air fryer zones, melt the butter.
5. Place the marinated shrimp in the same zone and air fry at 375°F (190°C) for about 5-6 minutes, or until the shrimp turn pink and opaque.
6. In the other zone, heat the cooked linguine pasta for about 2-3 minutes.
7. Toss the pasta and shrimp together before serving.
8. Serve your Shrimp Scampi hot and garnish with extra fresh parsley.
9. Enjoy your delicious seafood dish!

Air Fryer Salmon en Papillote

Serves 2 / Prep Time: 15 minutes / Cook Time: 15 minutes

- 2 salmon fillets (about 150g each)
- 100g asparagus spears
- 100g cherry tomatoes, halved
- 20g red onion, thinly sliced
- 10g fresh dill, chopped
- 10g olive oil
- 5g lemon juice
- Salt and black pepper to taste

1. Preheat your Ninja Foodi Dual Zone Air Fryer to 375°F (190°C) on the "Air Fry" setting.
2. Tear two large sheets of parchment paper (about 12x16 inches) for the papillote.
3. In a bowl, mix together the asparagus, cherry tomatoes, red onion, fresh dill, olive oil, lemon juice, salt, and black pepper.
4. Place the parchment paper sheets on a flat surface.
5. Divide the vegetable mixture equally between the two sheets, creating a bed for the salmon.
6. Place a salmon fillet on top of the vegetable mixture on each sheet.
7. Fold the parchment paper over the salmon and vegetables, then fold and crimp the edges to seal the packets.
8. Place the sealed packets in the air fryer basket.
9. Air fry at 375°F (190°C) for about 12-15 minutes, or until the salmon is cooked to your desired level (145°F/63°C for medium).
10. Carefully open the papillote packets to release the aromatic steam.
11. Serve your Salmon en Papillote hot and enjoy!

Air Fryer Lobster Tails

Serves 2 / Prep Time: 10 minutes / Cook Time: 15 minutes

- 2 lobster tails (about 150g each)
- 20g butter, melted
- 2 cloves garlic, minced
- 5g fresh parsley, chopped
- Salt and black pepper to taste
- Lemon wedges (for serving)

1. Preheat your Ninja Foodi Dual Zone Air Fryer to 375°F (190°C) on the "Air Fry" setting.
2. With kitchen shears, cut the top of the lobster shells lengthwise and pull the lobster meat up through the shell, leaving it attached at the tail.
3. Season the lobster tails with salt and black pepper.
4. In one of the air fryer zones, brush the lobster tails with melted butter and sprinkle with minced garlic.
5. Air fry at 375°F (190°C) for about 12-15 minutes, or until the lobster meat is opaque and slightly browned.
6. Garnish with chopped fresh parsley and serve with lemon wedges.
7. Enjoy your Air Fryer Lobster Tails.

Middle Eastern Za'atar Crusted Halibut

Serves: 2 / Prep time: 10 minutes / Cook time: 15 minutes

- 2 halibut fillets, about 150g each
- 1 tbsp za'atar
- 60g breadcrumbs
- 60g flour
- 1 egg, beaten
- Salt and black pepper, to taste
- Olive oil spray

1. Preheat the Ninja Dual Zone Air Fryer to 200°C on zone 1 for 5 minutes.
2. In a small bowl, mix together the za'atar, breadcrumbs, and flour.
3. Season the halibut fillets with salt and black pepper.
4. Dip each fillet in the beaten egg, then coat in the za'atar breadcrumb mixture, pressing it onto the fish to ensure it sticks.
5. Place the fillets on the crisper plate in zone 1 and lightly spray with olive oil.
6. Air fry at 200°C for 15 minutes or until the fish is cooked through and the crust is golden and crispy.

7. Once cooked, remove from the air fryer and serve immediately.

Moroccan Grilled Swordfish with Harissa

Serves: 4 / Prep time: 15 minutes / Marinate time: 30 minutes / Cook time: 10 minutes

- 4 swordfish steaks, about 150g each
- 2 tbsp harissa paste
- 1 tbsp olive oil
- 1 tsp ground cumin
- 1 tsp smoked paprika
- 1/2 tsp salt
- 1/4 tsp black pepper
- 1 lemon, cut into wedges

1. In a small bowl, mix together harissa paste, olive oil, ground cumin, smoked paprika, salt, and black pepper.
2. Place the swordfish steaks in a shallow dish or resealable plastic bag and coat with the harissa mixture. Cover and marinate in the refrigerator for at least 30 minutes, or up to 2 hours.
3. Preheat the Ninja Dual Zone Air Fryer to 200°C on zone 1 for 5 minutes.
4. Remove the swordfish from the marinade and discard any excess marinade.
5. Place the swordfish steaks on the crisper plate in zone 1 and air fry at 200°C for 8-10 minutes, flipping halfway through, or until the fish is cooked through and flakes easily with a fork.
6. Serve hot with lemon wedges on the side.

Cajun Shrimp and Sausage Foil Packets

Servings: 2 / Prep Time: 5 minutes / Cook Time: 12 minutes

- 300 grams large shrimp, peeled and deveined
- 200 grams smoked sausage, sliced
- 150 grams bell peppers, sliced
- 150 grams onion, sliced
- 2 cloves garlic, minced
- 30 grams Cajun seasoning
- 30 ml olive oil
- Salt and pepper, to taste
- Fresh parsley, chopped (for garnish)

1. Preheat your Air Fryer to 200°C.
2. Combine the shrimp, sausage, bell peppers, onion, minced garlic, Cajun seasoning, olive oil, salt, and pepper in a large bowl. Toss well to coat the ingredients evenly.
3. Divide the mixture into two equal portions and place each portion on a sheet of aluminum foil. Fold the foil over the ingredients, sealing the edges to create a packet.
4. Place the foil packets in the Ninja Dual Zone Air Fryer. Cook for 10-12 minutes or until the shrimp is cooked and the sausage is heated.
5. Carefully remove the foil packets from the air fryer and let them cool slightly before opening.
6. Sprinkle fresh parsley on top for garnish.
7. Serve the Cajun shrimp and sausage foil packets as a delicious and flavorful meal. You can enjoy them as they are or serve with rice or crusty bread.

Chimichurri Grilled Shrimp

Servings: 2 / Prep Time: 5 minutes / Cook Time: 12 minutes

- 400 g large shrimp, peeled and deveined
- 60 ml olive oil
- 30 ml red wine vinegar
- 15 g fresh parsley, finely chopped
- 15 g fresh cilantro, finely chopped
- 2 cloves garlic, minced
- 1 tablespoon lemon juice
- 1 teaspoon dried oregano
- 1/2 teaspoon red pepper flakes (adjust to taste)
- Salt and pepper, to taste
- Lemon wedges (for serving)

1. Preheat your Ninja Dual Zone Air Fryer to 200°C.
2. Combine the olive oil, red wine vinegar, chopped parsley, chopped cilantro, minced garlic, lemon juice, dried oregano, red pepper flakes, salt, and pepper in a bowl. Mix well to make the chimichurri marinade.
3. Add the shrimp to the marinade and toss to coat them evenly. Let the shrimp marinate for about 15 minutes to allow the flavors to infuse.
4. Once marinated, put the shrimp onto skewers, leaving a small space between each shrimp.
5. Place the shrimp skewers in the Ninja Dual Zone Air Fryer. Cook for 5-6 minutes, turning halfway through, or until the shrimp are cooked and slightly charred.
6. Remove the shrimp skewers from the air fryer and let them rest for a few minutes.
7. Serve the chimichurri grilled shrimp with lemon wedges on the side.

Lobster Mac and Cheese Bites

Serves: 6 / Prep time: 15 minutes / Cook time: 18 minutes

- 225g elbow macaroni
- 45g unsalted butter
- 45g plain flour
- 350ml whole milk
- 1 tsp garlic powder
- 1 tsp onion powder
- 1 tsp smoked paprika
- Salt and pepper, to taste
- 200g cooked lobster meat, chopped
- 115g sharp cheddar cheese, grated
- 50g panko breadcrumbs
- Cooking spray

1. Preheat the Ninja Dual Zone Air Fryer to 200°C using the "Bake" function.
2. Cook macaroni according to package instructions until al dente. Drain and set aside.
3. In a saucepan, melt butter over medium heat. Add flour and whisk constantly for 1-2 minutes.
4. Gradually whisk in milk until the mixture is smooth. Add garlic powder, onion powder, smoked paprika, salt and pepper.
5. Continue whisking until the mixture thickens and coats the back of a spoon.
6. Remove from heat and stir in the lobster meat and cheddar cheese until fully combined.
7. Add cooked macaroni and stir until well coated.
8. Grease a mini muffin tin with cooking spray. Spoon mac and cheese mixture into each cup.
9. Sprinkle panko breadcrumbs on top of each mac and cheese bite.
10. Place the muffin tin in zone 1 of the Ninja Dual Zone Air Fryer and select "Air Fry" for 8-10 minutes until the tops are golden brown and crispy.
11. Serve immediately.

Salmon Croquettes with Lemon-Dill Sauce

Serves: 4 / Prep time: 20 minutes / Cook time: 20 minutes

- 450g fresh salmon fillet, skin removed
- 60g panko breadcrumbs
- 60g mayonnaise
- 60g chopped green onions
- 1 egg, lightly beaten
- 1 tbsp Dijon mustard
- 1 tsp lemon zest
- 1/4 tsp salt
- 1/4 tsp black pepper
- 120g plain flour
- 120g panko breadcrumbs
- 2 tbsp olive oil
- For Lemon-Dill Sauce:
- 120g sour cream
- 2 tbsp fresh dill, chopped
- 1 tbsp lemon juice
- Salt and pepper, to taste

1. Preheat the Ninja Dual Zone Air Fryer to 200°C using the "Roast" function.
2. Cut salmon fillet into small pieces and pulse in a food processor until roughly chopped.
3. In a mixing bowl, combine the salmon, panko breadcrumbs, mayonnaise, green onions, egg, Dijon mustard, lemon zest, salt and black pepper. Mix well.
4. Use a tablespoon to form a mixture into small patties.
5. Place flour and panko breadcrumbs in separate shallow dishes.
6. Dredge each patty in flour, then in egg, and finally in panko breadcrumbs.
7. Brush the air fryer basket with olive oil and place the patties in zone 1 of the Ninja Dual Zone Air Fryer.
8. Roast for 10 minutes on each side or until golden brown and crispy.
9. While salmon croquettes are cooking, mix all ingredients for the lemon-dill sauce in a small bowl and set aside.
10. Serve salmon croquettes hot with lemon-dill sauce on the side.

Chapter 6 Sides and Appetizers

Air Fryer Chimichurri Chicken Thighs

Serves 2 / Prep Time: 20 minutes / Cook Time: 20 minutes

- For the Chimichurri Sauce:
- 1 cup fresh parsley (40g)
- 4 cloves garlic
- 1/4 cup red wine vinegar (60g)
- 1/4 cup olive oil (60g)
- 1 teaspoon dried oregano
- 1/2 teaspoon red pepper flakes (adjust to your spice preference)
- Salt and pepper to taste
- For the Chicken Thighs:
- 4 bone-in, skin-on chicken thighs (about 600g)
- Salt and pepper to taste

1. Start by preparing the Chimichurri Sauce. In a food processor, combine fresh parsley, garlic, red wine vinegar, olive oil, dried oregano, red pepper flakes, salt, and pepper. Pulse until the mixture is finely chopped and well combined.
2. Season the chicken thighs with salt and pepper, then rub them with about 1/4 cup of the prepared Chimichurri Sauce. Reserve the remaining sauce for serving.
3. Preheat your Ninja Foodi Dual Zone Air Fryer to 375°F (190°C).
4. Cooking the Chimichurri Chicken Thighs:
5. Place the seasoned chicken thighs in the air fryer basket.
6. Air fry at 375°F (190°C) for about 18-20 minutes, turning them once, until they are golden brown and cooked through with an internal temperature of 165°F (74°C).

Air Fryer Crab-Stuffed Mushrooms with Garlic Butter

Serves 2 / Prep Time: 15 minutes / Cook Time: 15 minutes

- For the Crab-Stuffed Mushrooms:
- 12 large white mushrooms
- 100g lump crabmeat
- 1/4 cup cream cheese (60g)
- 1/4 cup grated Parmesan cheese (30g)
- 1 green onion, finely chopped
- 1 clove garlic, minced
- Salt and pepper to taste
- For the Garlic Butter:
- 1/4 cup unsalted butter (60g)
- 2 cloves garlic, minced
- 1 tablespoon fresh parsley, chopped
- Salt and pepper to taste

1. Remove the stems from the mushrooms and clean them.
2. In a bowl, combine lump crabmeat, cream cheese, grated Parmesan cheese, chopped green onion, minced garlic, salt, and pepper. Mix well to form the crab stuffing.
3. Stuff each mushroom cap with the crab mixture.
4. Preheat your Ninja Foodi Dual Zone Air Fryer to 375°F (190°C).
5. Place the stuffed mushrooms in the air fryer basket.
6. Air fry at 375°F (190°C) for about 12-15 minutes until the mushrooms are tender, and the stuffing is heated through.
7. In a small saucepan, melt the unsalted butter. Add minced garlic, chopped fresh parsley, salt, and pepper. Cook for a couple of minutes until the garlic is fragrant.
8. Serve the Crab-Stuffed Mushrooms with a drizzle of the garlic butter.

Air Fryer Honey BBQ Chicken Sliders

Serves 2 / Prep Time: 15 minutes / Cook Time: 15 minutes

- For the Honey BBQ Chicken:
- 2 boneless, skinless chicken breasts (about 300g)
- Salt and black pepper to taste
- 1/2 cup barbecue sauce (120g)
- 2 tablespoons honey (30g)
- 1 teaspoon olive oil
- 1/2 teaspoon garlic powder
- 1/2 teaspoon onion powder
- 1/2 teaspoon paprika
- For the Sliders:
- 4 small slider buns
- 1/2 cup coleslaw (120g)
- Pickles for garnish (optional)

1. Season the chicken breasts with salt and black pepper.
2. In a bowl, combine barbecue sauce, honey, olive oil, garlic powder, onion powder, and paprika to create the honey BBQ sauce.

3. Preheat your air fryer to 375°F (190°C).
4. Brush the chicken breasts with the honey BBQ sauce.
5. Place the chicken breasts in the air fryer basket.
6. Air fry at 375°F (190°C) for about 12-15 minutes or until the chicken is cooked through and has an internal temperature of 165°F (74°C). Brush the chicken with more sauce halfway through the cooking time.
7. Let the chicken rest for a few minutes before slicing it into slider-sized pieces.
8. Slice the slider buns in half and toast them in the air fryer for a minute or two, cut side up.
9. Place a portion of honey BBQ chicken on the bottom half of each bun.
10. Top with coleslaw and pickles if desired.
11. Place the top half of the buns on each slider.

Crispy Fried Asparagus and Prosciutto Bundles

Serves 2 / Prep Time: 20 minutes / Cook Time: 12 minutes

- For the Asparagus Bundles:
- 200g fresh asparagus spears, trimmed
- 4 slices of prosciutto
- 2 tablespoons olive oil
- Salt and black pepper to taste
- For the Lemon Garlic Aioli:
- 1/2 cup mayonnaise (115g)
- 1 clove garlic, minced
- Zest and juice of 1 lemon
- 1 teaspoon Dijon mustard
- Salt and black pepper to taste

1. Preheat your Ninja Foodi Dual Zone Air Fryer to 375°F (190°C).
2. Divide the asparagus into two equal portions and wrap each portion with 2 slices of prosciutto. Drizzle olive oil over the bundles and season with salt and black pepper.
3. Place the asparagus bundles in the air fryer basket.
4. Air fry at 375°F (190°C) for about 10-12 minutes until the asparagus is tender and the prosciutto is crispy.
5. In a small bowl, combine mayonnaise, minced garlic, lemon zest, lemon juice, Dijon mustard, salt, and black pepper. Mix well.
6. Serve the Crispy Fried Asparagus and Prosciutto Bundles with the Lemon Garlic Aioli for dipping.

Korean BBQ Chicken Wings

Serves 2 / Prep Time: 15 minutes / Cook Time: 30 minutes

- 500g chicken wings
- 1/4 cup soy sauce (60g)
- 1/4 cup brown sugar (60g)
- 3 cloves garlic, minced
- 1 tablespoon fresh ginger, grated
- 1 tablespoon sesame oil
- 1 tablespoon rice vinegar
- 1 tablespoon Gochujang (Korean chili paste)
- 1 green onion, chopped (for garnish)
- Toasted sesame seeds (for garnish)

1. In a bowl, mix together soy sauce, brown sugar, minced garlic, grated ginger, sesame oil, rice vinegar, and Gochujang to create the marinade for the chicken wings.
2. Place the chicken wings in a large zip-top bag or a bowl. Pour the marinade over the wings, seal the bag, and toss to coat the wings. Marinate for at least 15 minutes, or longer if desired.
3. Preheat your Air fryer to 425°F (220°C).
4. Line a baking sheet with aluminum foil and place a wire rack on top. Spray the rack with cooking spray.
5. Remove the chicken wings from the marinade, allowing any excess to drip off, and place them on the wire rack.
6. Bake the wings in the preheated oven for about 30 minutes, turning them halfway through, until they are cooked through and crispy.
7. While the wings are cooking, you can brush them with more of the marinade to build up the flavor if desired.
8. Once the wings are done, transfer them to a serving plate.
9. Garnish with chopped green onions and toasted sesame seeds.
10. Serve your Korean BBQ chicken wings hot with your favorite dipping sauce.

Air Fryer Lemon Pepper Chicken Wings

Serves 2 / Prep Time: 10 minutes / Cook Time: 20 minutes

- For the Chicken Wings:
- 500g chicken wings
- 1/4 cup all-purpose flour (30g)
- 1 tablespoon lemon pepper seasoning
- 1 teaspoon salt
- For Lemon Pepper Sauce:
- 2 tablespoons melted butter
- 1 tablespoon lemon juice
- 1/2 teaspoon lemon pepper seasoning

1. In a bowl, mix the all-purpose flour, lemon pepper seasoning, and salt to create the coating for the chicken wings.

2. Toss the chicken wings in the flour mixture until they are well coated.
3. Preheat your air fryer to 375°F (190°C).
4. Place the coated chicken wings in the air fryer basket in a single layer. You may need to cook them in batches if they don't all fit without crowding.
5. Air fry the wings at 375°F (190°C) for about 20 minutes, turning them halfway through, or until they are golden brown and crispy.
6. In a small bowl, whisk together the melted butter, lemon juice, and additional lemon pepper seasoning.
7. Toss the cooked chicken wings in the lemon pepper sauce for an extra burst of flavor.

Crispy Fried Brussels Sprout and Bacon Salad

Serves 2 / Prep Time: 15 minutes / Cook Time: 15 minutes

- For the Salad:
- 200g Brussels sprouts, trimmed and halved
- 100g bacon, chopped
- 50g red onion, thinly sliced
- 50g pecans, chopped
- 50g dried cranberries
- 50g feta cheese, crumbled
- For the Dressing:
- 2 tablespoons olive oil
- 1 tablespoon balsamic vinegar
- 1 teaspoon honey
- Salt and pepper to taste

1. Preheat your air fryer to 375°F (190°C).
2. In a bowl, toss the halved Brussels sprouts with a little olive oil, salt, and pepper.
3. Place the Brussels sprouts in the air fryer basket and cook for 12-15 minutes or until they are crispy and slightly browned. Shake the basket occasionally for even cooking.
4. While the Brussels sprouts are cooking, cook the chopped bacon in a skillet over medium heat until crispy. Remove and drain on paper towels.
5. In a small bowl, whisk together the olive oil, balsamic vinegar, honey, salt, and pepper to create the dressing.
6. Once the Brussels sprouts are done, transfer them to a large mixing bowl.
7. Add the crispy bacon, thinly sliced red onion, chopped pecans, dried cranberries, and crumbled feta cheese to the bowl with the Brussels sprouts.
8. Drizzle the dressing over the salad and toss everything to combine.
9. Serve immediately as a warm salad or let it cool for a few minutes before serving.

Air Fryer Crab Rangoon Dip

Serves 2 / Prep Time: 15 minutes / Cook Time: 12 minutes

- 200g cream cheese, softened
- 100g imitation crab meat, finely chopped
- 2 green onions, finely chopped
- 1/4 cup mayonnaise (60g)
- 1/4 cup sour cream (60g)
- 1/4 cup shredded mozzarella cheese (60g)
- 1/4 cup grated Parmesan cheese (60g)
- 1/2 teaspoon Worcestershire sauce
- 1/2 teaspoon garlic powder
- Salt and pepper to taste

1. In a mixing bowl, combine the softened cream cheese, finely chopped imitation crab meat, chopped green onions, mayonnaise, sour cream, mozzarella cheese, Parmesan cheese, Worcestershire sauce, garlic powder, salt, and pepper. Mix until all the ingredients are well combined.
2. Preheat your Ninja Foodi Dual Zone Air Fryer to 350°F (175°C).
3. Transfer the crab Rangoon dip mixture to an oven-safe dish that fits inside the air fryer basket.
4. Place the dish in the air fryer basket and cook at 350°F (175°C) for about 12 minutes or until the top is bubbly and golden brown.
5. Carefully remove the dish from the air fryer using oven mitts or tongs.
6. Serve the hot crab Rangoon dip with your favorite dippers, such as wonton chips or fresh vegetables.

Fried Goat Cheese Salad with Candied Pecans and Raspberry Vinaigrette

Serves 2 / Prep Time: 15 minutes / Cook Time: 10 minutes

- For the Salad:
- 100g goat cheese, cut into 4 discs
- 100g mixed salad greens
- 50g candied pecans
- 50g cherry tomatoes, halved
- 50g red onion, thinly sliced
- For the Goat Cheese Coating:
- 50g all-purpose flour
- 1 egg, beaten
- 50g breadcrumbs
- 1/2 teaspoon dried thyme
- Salt and pepper to taste
- For the Raspberry Vinaigrette:
- 1/4 cup fresh raspberries (60g)
- 2 tablespoons olive oil
- 2 tablespoons red wine vinegar

- 1 teaspoon honey
- Salt and pepper to taste

1. Start by preparing the Raspberry Vinaigrette. In a small blender, combine fresh raspberries, olive oil, red wine vinegar, honey, salt, and pepper. Blend until smooth. Set the vinaigrette aside.
2. In three separate bowls, place the all-purpose flour in one, the beaten egg in another, and mix the breadcrumbs with dried thyme, salt, and pepper in the third.
3. Dip each goat cheese disc into the flour, then the beaten egg, and finally coat them in the breadcrumb mixture. Place them on a plate.
4. Preheat your oven to 350°F (175°C).
5. In a large skillet, heat some olive oil over medium heat. Once hot, add the goat cheese discs and cook for about 1-2 minutes on each side until golden brown. Transfer them to the preheated oven for 5 minutes to ensure they're melty on the inside.
6. While the goat cheese is in the oven, assemble the salad. Toss the mixed salad greens, candied pecans, cherry tomatoes, and thinly sliced red onion together.
7. Divide the salad mixture onto two plates.
8. Place the warm, crispy fried goat cheese discs on top of the salad.
9. Drizzle the Raspberry Vinaigrette over the salad.
10. Serve immediately and enjoy!

Sweet and Spicy Chicken Wings

Serves 2 / Prep Time: 15 minutes / Cook Time: 25 minutes

- For the Chicken Wings:
- 400g chicken wings, split into drumettes and flats
- 5g salt
- 5g black pepper
- 5g paprika
- 5g garlic powder
- 5g onion powder
- For the Sweet and Spicy Sauce:
- 30g honey
- 20g hot sauce
- 10g ketchup
- 10g soy sauce
- 5g minced garlic
- 5g minced ginger

1. In a bowl, season the chicken wings with salt, black pepper, paprika, garlic powder, and onion powder. Toss to coat evenly.
2. Preheat your Ninja Foodi Dual Zone Air Fryer to 400°F (200°C) using the "Air Fry" setting.
3. Place the seasoned chicken wings in the air fryer basket in a single layer.
4. Air fry for about 25 minutes, flipping the wings halfway through, until they are crispy and cooked through.
5. While the chicken wings are cooking, prepare the sauce. In a saucepan, combine honey, hot sauce, ketchup, soy sauce, minced garlic, and minced ginger. Heat over low heat until the sauce is heated through.
6. Once the wings are done, toss them in the sweet and spicy sauce until well-coated.

Crispy Fried Mushrooms

Serves 2 / Prep Time: 15 minutes / Cook Time: 10 minutes

- 200g button mushrooms
- 100g all-purpose flour
- 5g garlic powder
- 5g onion powder
- 5g salt
- 5g black pepper
- 1 egg
- Cooking oil, for frying

1. Preheat your Ninja Foodi Dual Zone Air Fryer to 375°F (190°C) using the "Air Fry" setting.
2. In a bowl, combine the all-purpose flour, garlic powder, onion powder, salt, and black pepper.
3. In another bowl, beat the egg.
4. Dip each mushroom into the egg, then into the flour mixture, ensuring they are well-coated.
5. Lightly brush the air fryer basket with cooking oil.
6. Place the coated mushrooms in the air fryer basket.
7. Air fry for about 8-10 minutes or until the mushrooms are golden and crispy.
8. Remove from the air fryer and let them cool slightly before serving.

Sesame Chicken Wings

Serves 2 / Prep Time: 20 minutes / Cook Time: 20 minutes

- For the Chicken Wings:
- 400g chicken wings, split into drumettes and flats
- 30g soy sauce
- 15g honey
- 10g sesame oil
- 5g garlic powder
- 5g ground ginger
- 5g black pepper
- Sesame seeds for garnish

1. In a bowl, mix together soy sauce, honey, sesame oil, garlic powder, ground ginger, and black pepper

to make the marinade.
2. Place the chicken wings in a zip-top bag or shallow dish and pour the marinade over them. Seal the bag or cover the dish and marinate for at least 30 minutes, or overnight in the refrigerator.
3. Preheat your Ninja Foodi Dual Zone Air Fryer to 375°F (190°C) using the "Air Fry" setting.
4. Lightly grease the air fryer basket.
5. Remove the chicken wings from the marinade and place them in the air fryer basket.
6. Air fry for about 18-20 minutes, flipping them over halfway through, until they are crispy and cooked through.
7. While the chicken wings are cooking, sprinkle sesame seeds over them for garnish.

Air Fryer Orange Chicken

Serves 2 / Prep Time: 15 minutes / Cook Time: 15 minutes

- 400g boneless, skinless chicken thighs, cut into bite-sized pieces
- 60g all-purpose flour
- 30g cornstarch
- 5g salt
- 5g black pepper
- Cooking oil spray
- Sesame seeds, for garnish (optional)
- Sliced green onions, for garnish (optional)
- For the Orange Sauce:
- 120ml orange juice
- 30ml soy sauce
- 30ml rice vinegar
- 30g granulated sugar
- 5g orange zest
- 5g minced ginger
- 5g minced garlic
- 5g cornstarch mixed with 10ml water (cornstarch slurry)

1. In a bowl, combine the all-purpose flour, cornstarch, salt, and black pepper.
2. Lightly coat the chicken pieces in this mixture, shaking off any excess.
3. Preheat your Ninja Foodi Dual Zone Air Fryer to 375°F (190°C) using the "Air Fry" setting.
4. Lightly grease the air fryer basket with cooking oil spray.
5. Arrange the coated chicken pieces in a single layer in the air fryer basket.
6. Air fry for about 10-12 minutes, flipping the chicken pieces halfway through, or until they are golden and crispy. You may need to cook in batches if your air fryer has a smaller basket.
7. While the chicken is cooking, make the orange sauce. In a small saucepan, combine orange juice, soy sauce, rice vinegar, granulated sugar, orange zest, minced ginger, and minced garlic.
8. Bring the sauce to a simmer over medium heat. Once it's simmering, add the cornstarch slurry and continue to cook, stirring constantly until the sauce thickens. This should take about 2-3 minutes.
9. Once the chicken is done, transfer it to a large bowl.
10. Pour the orange sauce over the crispy chicken and toss to coat the chicken evenly.
11. Garnish with sesame seeds and sliced green onions, if desired.

Teriyaki Chicken Wings

Serves 2 / Prep Time: 15 minutes / Cook Time: 25 minutes

- For the Chicken Wings:
- 400g chicken wings, split into drumettes and flats
- 5g garlic powder
- 5g ginger, minced
- 60ml soy sauce
- 60ml mirin
- 30g brown sugar
- 2g sesame seeds (optional)

1. In a bowl, combine garlic powder, minced ginger, soy sauce, mirin, and brown sugar to make the teriyaki sauce.
2. Place the chicken wings in a zip-top bag or shallow dish and pour half of the teriyaki sauce over them. Seal the bag or cover the dish and marinate for at least 30 minutes, or overnight in the refrigerator.
3. Preheat your Ninja Foodi Dual Zone Air Fryer to 400°F (200°C) using the "Air Fry" setting.
4. Lightly grease the air fryer basket.
5. Remove the chicken wings from the marinade and place them in the air fryer basket.
6. Air fry for about 20-25 minutes, turning them over halfway through, until they are crispy and cooked through.
7. While the chicken wings are cooking, you can heat the remaining teriyaki sauce in a small saucepan until it thickens.
8. Once the chicken wings are done, toss them in the thickened teriyaki sauce, and garnish with sesame seeds (optional).

Crispy Fried Tofu Nuggets

Serves 2 / Prep Time: 20 minutes / Cook Time: 15 minutes

- 300g extra-firm tofu, pressed and cut into nugget-sized pieces

- 50g cornstarch
- 5g garlic powder
- 5g onion powder
- 5g salt
- 5g black pepper
- 1 egg
- Cooking oil, for frying

1. In a bowl, combine the cornstarch, garlic powder, onion powder, salt, and black pepper.
2. In another bowl, beat the egg.
3. Dip each tofu nugget into the egg, then into the cornstarch mixture, ensuring they are well-coated.
4. Preheat your Ninja Foodi Dual Zone Air Fryer to 375°F (190°C) using the "Air Fry" setting.
5. Lightly grease the air fryer basket with cooking oil.
6. Place the coated tofu nuggets in the air fryer basket.
7. Air fry for about 12-15 minutes, turning them over halfway through, until they are golden and crispy.
8. Remove from the air fryer and let them cool slightly before serving.

Coconut Shrimp Salad

Serves 2 / Prep Time: 20 minutes / Cook Time: 10 minutes

- For the Coconut Shrimp:
- 200g large shrimp, peeled and deveined
- 50g shredded coconut
- 50g breadcrumbs
- 2g salt
- 2g black pepper
- 1 egg
- Cooking oil, for frying
- For the Salad:
- 150g mixed greens
- 50g diced pineapple
- 50g diced red bell pepper
- 50g cherry tomatoes, halved
- 30g sliced red onion
- 30g toasted coconut flakes
- 30ml vinaigrette dressing

1. In a bowl, combine shredded coconut and breadcrumbs. Season with salt and black pepper.
2. In another bowl, beat the egg.
3. Dredge each shrimp in the breadcrumb and coconut mixture, then dip it in the beaten egg, and coat it again with the breadcrumb mixture, pressing the breadcrumbs onto the shrimp to adhere.
4. Preheat your Ninja Foodi Dual Zone Air Fryer to 375°F (190°C) using the "Air Fry" setting.
5. Lightly grease the air fryer basket with cooking oil.
6. Place the breaded shrimp in the air fryer basket.
7. Air fry for about 8-10 minutes or until the shrimp are golden and crispy.
8. While the shrimp is cooking, prepare the salad by combining mixed greens, diced pineapple, diced red bell pepper, cherry tomatoes, sliced red onion, and toasted coconut flakes in a large salad bowl.
9. Once the shrimp is done, add them to the salad and drizzle vinaigrette dressing over the top.

Air Fryer Crab-Stuffed Mushrooms

Serves 2 / Prep Time: 15 minutes / Cook Time: 15 minutes

- 150g lump crabmeat
- 100g cream cheese, softened
- 30g grated Parmesan cheese
- 2g garlic powder
- 2g onion powder
- 4 large mushrooms
- Cooking oil, for brushing
- 5g fresh parsley, chopped (for garnish)

1. In a bowl, mix lump crabmeat, softened cream cheese, grated Parmesan cheese, garlic powder, and onion powder until well combined.
2. Remove the stems from the mushrooms and brush the caps lightly with cooking oil.
3. Preheat your Ninja Foodi Dual Zone Air Fryer to 375°F (190°C) using the "Air Fry" setting.
4. Stuff each mushroom cap with the crab and cheese mixture.
5. Place the stuffed mushrooms in the air fryer basket.
6. Air fry for about 12-15 minutes or until the mushrooms are tender and the filling is hot and slightly golden.
7. Garnish with chopped fresh parsley before serving.

Fried Green Tomato BLT

Serves 2 / Prep Time: 20 minutes / Cook Time: 10 minutes

- For the Fried Green Tomatoes:
- 2 large green tomatoes, sliced into rounds
- 100g cornmeal
- 5g paprika
- 5g salt
- 5g black pepper
- 1 egg
- Cooking oil, for frying
- For the BLT Assembly:
- 4 slices of bacon, cooked
- 4 large lettuce leaves
- 4 slices of bread
- 60g mayonnaise
- 60g sliced red onion

- 60g sliced ripe tomatoes

1. In a bowl, combine cornmeal, paprika, salt, and black pepper.
2. In another bowl, beat the egg.
3. Dredge each green tomato slice in the cornmeal mixture, then dip it in the beaten egg, and coat it again with the cornmeal mixture, pressing the mixture onto the tomato to adhere.
4. Preheat your Ninja Foodi Dual Zone Air Fryer to 375°F (190°C) using the "Air Fry" setting.
5. Lightly grease the air fryer basket with cooking oil.
6. Place the coated green tomato slices in the air fryer basket.
7. Air fry for about 8-10 minutes or until the tomatoes are golden and crispy.
8. While the tomatoes are cooking, prepare the BLT sandwiches. Spread mayonnaise on each slice of bread. Layer lettuce, bacon, sliced red onion, fried green tomato slices, and ripe tomato slices to make the sandwiches.

Air Fryer Spicy Chicken Tenders

Serves 2 / Prep Time: 20 minutes / Cook Time: 12 minutes

- 300g chicken tenders
- 50g breadcrumbs
- 5g paprika
- 5g garlic powder
- 5g onion powder
- 5g cayenne pepper
- Salt and black pepper to taste
- Cooking spray

1. In a bowl, mix breadcrumbs, paprika, garlic powder, onion powder, cayenne pepper, salt, and black pepper.
2. Dredge the chicken tenders in the breadcrumb mixture, ensuring they are evenly coated.
3. Preheat your Ninja Foodi Dual Zone Air Fryer to 375°F (190°C).
4. Spray the air fryer basket with cooking spray and place the breaded chicken tenders inside, ensuring they are not touching.
5. Air fry at 375°F (190°C) for 10-12 minutes, or until the chicken tenders are golden brown and cooked through.

Korean Fried Chicken (Yangnyeom Chicken)

Serves 2 / Prep Time: 20 minutes / Cook Time: 30 minutes

- 400g chicken wings
- 70g potato starch
- 1/2 tsp salt
- 1/4 tsp black pepper
- 2 large eggs
- Cooking spray
- For the Yangnyeom Sauce:
- 2 tbsp gochujang (Korean red pepper paste)
- 1 1/2 tbsp soy sauce
- 1 1/2 tbsp honey
- 1 tbsp rice vinegar
- 1 tbsp brown sugar
- 1 tsp grated ginger
- 1 tsp minced garlic
- 1 tsp sesame oil

1. Preheat the Ninja Foodi Dual Zone Air Fryer to 400°F (200°C) using the "Air Fry" setting.
2. In a large mixing bowl, combine the potato starch, salt, and black pepper.
3. Beat the eggs in a separate bowl.
4. Dip each chicken wing into the beaten eggs and then coat it with the potato starch mixture. Repeat this process for a thicker crust if desired.
5. Place the coated chicken wings in the Ninja Foodi Dual Zone Air Fryer basket, making sure not to overcrowd the basket. Spray the wings lightly with cooking spray.
6. Put the chicken wings in the Dual Zone Air Fryer, ensuring they are in a single layer.
7. Set the Dual Zone Air Fryer to Air Fry at 400°F (200°C) for 25 minutes. Cook until the chicken is golden brown and crispy, flipping the wings halfway through the cooking time.
8. While the chicken is cooking, prepare the Yangnyeom sauce. In a saucepan, combine all the sauce ingredients and heat over low heat, stirring until the sauce thickens. Remove from heat.
9. Once the chicken is done, remove it from the Air Fryer, place it in a large bowl, and drizzle the Yangnyeom sauce over the wings. Toss the wings to coat them evenly with the sauce.
10. Serve hot, garnished with sesame seeds and chopped green onions.

Fried Jalapeno Popper Dip

Serves 2 / Prep Time: 20 minutes / Cook Time: 10 minutes

- 100g cream cheese
- 50g sour cream
- 50g mayonnaise
- 50g shredded cheddar cheese
- 50g diced jalapenos

- 30g grated Parmesan cheese
- 5g minced garlic
- 5g breadcrumbs
- Cooking spray

1. In a bowl, mix cream cheese, sour cream, mayonnaise, cheddar cheese, diced jalapenos, grated Parmesan, and minced garlic until well combined.
2. Transfer the mixture to an oven-safe dish and top it with breadcrumbs.
3. Preheat your Ninja Foodi Dual Zone Air Fryer to 375°F (190°C).
4. Spray the air fryer basket with cooking spray and place the dish with the dip inside.
5. Air fry at 375°F (190°C) for 8-10 minutes or until the dip is hot and bubbly, and the top is golden brown.

Air Fryer Chicken Liver Pâté

Serves 2 / Prep Time: 15 minutes / Cook Time: 15 minutes

- 200g chicken livers
- 30g shallots, chopped
- 5g garlic, minced
- 30g butter
- 20ml brandy
- 50ml heavy cream
- 2g fresh thyme leaves
- Salt and pepper, to taste

1. Preheat your Ninja Foodi Dual Zone Air Fryer to 375°F (190°C) on the "Air Fry" setting.
2. Clean and trim the chicken livers, removing any connective tissues.
3. In a bowl, mix the cleaned chicken livers with salt and pepper.
4. In one air fryer zone, place the seasoned chicken livers.
5. Air fry at 375°F (190°C) for about 8-10 minutes, turning them once, until they are cooked through but slightly pink in the center.
6. In the other air fryer zone, heat butter and sauté chopped shallots and minced garlic until translucent.
7. Add fresh thyme leaves and brandy to the shallot mixture and cook for a couple of minutes.
8. Combine the sautéed shallot mixture with the air-fried chicken livers in a food processor.
9. Add heavy cream and blend until the mixture becomes smooth.
10. Adjust the seasoning if needed.
11. Transfer the chicken liver pâté into ramekins or jars.
12. Chill in the refrigerator for at least 2 hours before serving.
13. Enjoy your Air Fryer Chicken Liver Pâté with crackers or crusty bread!

Fried Plantains

Serves 2 / Prep Time: 10 minutes / Cook Time: 15 minutes

- 2 ripe plantains (approximately 200g each)
- 30g vegetable oil
- 1/2 tsp salt
- Cooking spray

1. Peel the ripe plantains and cut them into 1-inch thick diagonal slices.
2. In a large bowl, toss the plantain slices with vegetable oil and salt until they are well coated.
3. Preheat the Ninja Foodi Dual Zone Air Fryer to 375°F (190°C) using the "Air Fry" setting.
4. Place the plantain slices in the Dual Zone Air Fryer basket, ensuring they are in a single layer and not overcrowded.
5. Spray the plantain slices lightly with cooking spray.
6. Set the Dual Zone Air Fryer to Air Fry at 375°F (190°C) for 12-15 minutes or until the plantains are golden brown and crispy.
7. Serve hot as a side dish or snack.

Air Fryer Sesame Ginger Tofu

Serves 2 / Prep Time: 30 minutes / Cook Time: 15 minutes

- 300g extra-firm tofu, cubed
- 10g sesame oil
- 10g soy sauce
- 5g rice vinegar
- 5g honey
- 5g minced ginger
- 5g sesame seeds
- 10g cornstarch
- Cooking spray

1. In a bowl, mix sesame oil, soy sauce, rice vinegar, honey, minced ginger, and sesame seeds to make the marinade.
2. Toss the tofu cubes in the marinade and let them sit for 20 minutes.
3. Toss the marinated tofu cubes in cornstarch to coat them evenly.
4. Preheat your Ninja Foodi Dual Zone Air Fryer to 375°F (190°C).
5. Spray the air fryer basket with cooking spray and place the tofu cubes inside.
6. Air fry at 375°F (190°C) for 12-15 minutes, shaking the basket halfway through, until the tofu is crispy and golden.

Air Fryer Onion Rings

Serves 2 / Prep Time: 15 minutes / Cook Time: 10 minutes

- 200g yellow onions, sliced into rings
- 100g all-purpose flour
- 2 eggs, beaten
- 100g breadcrumbs
- 5g paprika
- 5g garlic powder
- Salt and black pepper to taste
- Cooking spray

1. In a bowl, combine the breadcrumbs, paprika, garlic powder, salt, and black pepper.
2. Dredge the onion rings in flour, dip them in beaten eggs, and coat with the breadcrumb mixture.
3. Preheat your Ninja Foodi Dual Zone Air Fryer to 375°F (190°C).
4. Place the breaded onion rings in the air fryer basket, making sure they are not touching.
5. Air fry at 375°F (190°C) for 8-10 minutes, or until they are crispy and golden brown.

Air Fryer Garlic Parmesan Wings

Serves 2 / Prep Time: 10 minutes / Cook Time: 25 minutes

- 10 chicken wings (about 400g)
- 20g olive oil
- 5g garlic powder
- 5g onion powder
- 5g dried oregano
- 5g dried basil
- 5g salt
- 5g black pepper
- 50g grated Parmesan cheese
- Fresh parsley for garnish

1. Preheat your Ninja Foodi Dual Zone Air Fryer to 375°F (190°C) on the "Air Fry" setting.
2. In a bowl, mix the chicken wings with olive oil, garlic powder, onion powder, dried oregano, dried basil, salt, and black pepper. Toss to coat.
3. In one air fryer zone, place the seasoned chicken wings.
4. Air fry at 375°F (190°C) for about 20-25 minutes, turning them once or twice during cooking, until the wings are golden brown and crispy.
5. In the last few minutes, sprinkle the grated Parmesan cheese over the wings and allow it to melt.
6. Garnish with fresh parsley before serving.
7. Serve your Garlic Parmesan Wings hot with your favorite dipping sauce.
8. Enjoy these flavorful, crispy wings!

Pakoras (Indian Vegetable Fritters)

Serves 2 / Prep Time: 20 minutes / Cook Time: 15 minutes

- 150g chickpea flour (besan)
- 1/2 tsp ground cumin
- 1/2 tsp ground coriander
- 1/4 tsp red chili powder
- 1/4 tsp turmeric
- 1/2 tsp salt
- 1/4 tsp baking soda
- 150ml water
- 200g mixed vegetables (e. g. , potatoes, onions, bell peppers, spinach) thinly sliced
- Cooking spray
- Mint chutney or tamarind sauce for dipping (optional)

1. In a mixing bowl, combine chickpea flour, ground cumin, ground coriander, red chili powder, turmeric, salt, and baking soda.
2. Gradually add water while whisking to create a smooth, lump-free batter.
3. Add the sliced vegetables to the batter and coat them evenly.
4. Preheat the Ninja Foodi Dual Zone Air Fryer to 375°F (190°C) using the "Air Fry" setting.
5. Place the coated vegetable slices in the Dual Zone Air Fryer basket, ensuring they are in a single layer and not overcrowded.
6. Spray the vegetables with cooking spray.
7. Set the Dual Zone Air Fryer to Air Fry at 375°F (190°C) for 10-15 minutes or until the Pakoras are crispy and golden brown.
8. Serve hot with mint chutney or tamarind sauce, if desired.

Stuffed Mushrooms

Prep time: 10 minutes / Cook time: 13 minutes / Serves 4

- 8 medium portobello mushrooms
- 50g butter, room temperature
- 180g feta cheese, pressed and crumbled
- 1 bell pepper, seeded and chopped
- 1 garlic clove, minced
- 2 scallion stalks, chopped
- Sea salt and ground black pepper, to taste
- 1 tbsp olive oil

1. Insert crisper plates in both drawers. Spray the crisper plates with nonstick cooking oil.
2. Pat the mushrooms dry with paper (or tea) towels and remove the stems; chop the stems and reserve.
3. Add the mushroom stems, butter, cheese, bell

pepper, garlic, scallions, salt, and black pepper to a mixing bowl. Stir to combine and divide the filling between portobello mushrooms.
4. Place the stuffed mushrooms in both drawers and brush them with olive oil.
5. Select zone 1 and pair it with "AIR FRY" at 185°C for 13 minutes. Select "MATCH" followed by the "START/STOP" button.
6. Bon appétit!

Potato Latkes

Prep time: 10 minutes / Cook time: 15 minutes / Serves 4

- 4 large potatoes, scrubbed
- 1 onion, peeled and chopped
- 1 garlic clove, minced
- 2 medium eggs, beaten
- 4 tbsp plain flour
- 1 tbsp cilanotro (or parsley)
- 1 tbsp rosemary
- Sea salt and ground black pepper, to taste
- 1 tbsp olive oil

1. Insert crisper plates in both drawers. Spray the crisper plates with nonstick cooking oil.
2. Coarsely grate your potatoes with skin. Now, wring out the liquid with a clean tea towel. (Maris Piper potatoes work best).
3. Add the other ingredients to the grated potatoes. Shape the mixture into latkes, flattening gently with a wide spatula (or fork).
4. Arrange potato lathes in both drawers of your Ninja Foodi.
5. Select zone 1 and pair it with "AIR FRY" at 180°C for 15 minutes. Select "MATCH" followed by the "START/STOP" button. Flip potato latkes halfway through the cooking time.
6. Bon appétit!

Cauliflower Buffalo Bites

Serves: 4-6 / Prep time: 10 minutes / Cook time: 10-12 minutes

- 1 head of cauliflower, cut into small florets
- 64g all-purpose flour
- 1 tsp garlic powder
- 1/2 tsp smoked paprika
- 1/2 tsp salt
- 1/2 tsp black pepper
- 64g buffalo sauce
- 2 tbsp melted butter

1. Preheat the Ninja Dual Zone to Air Fry at 190°C.
2. In a bowl, mix the flour, garlic powder, smoked paprika, salt, and black pepper.
3. Add the cauliflower florets to the bowl and toss until they are coated in the flour mixture.
4. Place the cauliflower in the air fryer basket and Air Fry at 190°C for 10-12 minutes until they are crispy and golden brown.
5. In a separate bowl, mix the buffalo sauce and melted butter.
6. Toss the cooked cauliflower in the buffalo sauce mixture until they are coated.
7. Serve hot.

Mini Cornish Pasties

Serves: 6-8 / Prep time: 30 minutes / Cook time: 25-30 minutes

- 320g of all-purpose flour
- 1/2 tsp salt
- 1/2 tsp baking powder
- 64g unsalted butter, chilled and diced
- 64g vegetable shortening, chilled and diced
- 60 ml of cold water
- 1 egg, beaten
- 1 large potato, peeled and diced
- 1 large carrot, peeled and diced
- 1 small onion, peeled and diced
- 128g cooked diced beef
- Salt and pepper, to taste
- 1 tbsp butter, diced

1. Preheat your Ninja Dual Zone to 190°C (190°C) on Air Fry mode.
2. In a large bowl, whisk together flour, salt, and baking powder. Using a pastry blender, cut in butter and shorten until the mixture resembles coarse crumbs.
3. Add cold water and stir until a dough forms. Turn out onto a floured surface and knead for 1-2 minutes until smooth. Divide dough into 8 equal portions and roll each into a ball.
4. In a separate bowl, combine diced potato, carrot, onion, and cooked beef. Season with salt and pepper to taste.
5. On a floured surface, roll each ball of dough into a 5-inch circle. Spoon 32g of the beef and vegetable mixture onto one half of each circle. Dot with butter.
6. Fold the other half of the dough over the filling and crimp the edges together to seal. Brush the beaten egg over the pasties.
7. Place the pasties in the Ninja Dual Zone on Air Fry mode for 18-20 minutes or until golden brown and crispy.

Chapter 7 Veggie and Vegetarian

Fried Avocado and Black Bean Quesadillas

Serves 2 / Prep Time: 15 minutes / Cook Time: 15 minutes

- For the Quesadillas:
- 2 large flour tortillas (about 200g)
- 1 ripe avocado, sliced
- 1 cup canned black beans, drained and rinsed (130g)
- 1 cup shredded cheddar cheese (120g)
- 1/4 cup chopped fresh cilantro (15g)
- 1/4 cup diced red onion (30g)
- 1 teaspoon ground cumin
- Salt and pepper to taste
- Vegetable oil for frying
- For the Dipping Sauce:
- 1/2 cup sour cream (120g)
- 1 tablespoon lime juice
- 1 teaspoon chili powder
- 1/2 teaspoon garlic powder
- Salt to taste

1. In a bowl, mash the black beans with a fork, then stir in the ground cumin, chopped cilantro, diced red onion, salt, and pepper. Mix well.
2. In another bowl, prepare the dipping sauce by combining sour cream, lime juice, chili powder, garlic powder, and a pinch of salt. Mix until smooth.
3. Lay out one flour tortilla, then spread half of the black bean mixture on one half of the tortilla. On top of the beans, add half of the avocado slices and half of the shredded cheddar cheese. Fold the other half of the tortilla over the fillings.
4. Repeat this process with the second tortilla.
5. Preheat a large skillet over medium heat and add a bit of vegetable oil.
6. Carefully place one quesadilla in the skillet and cook for about 2-3 minutes on each side until they are golden brown and the cheese is melted. Repeat the process with the second quesadilla.
7. Once cooked, cut each quesadilla into wedges.

Crispy Fried Brussels Sprout Caesar Salad

Serves 2 / Prep Time: 15 minutes / Cook Time: 10 minutes

- For the Crispy Fried Brussels Sprouts:
- 200g Brussels sprouts, trimmed and halved
- 1/4 cup all-purpose flour (30g)
- 2 large eggs, beaten
- 1/2 cup panko breadcrumbs (60g)
- 1/4 cup grated Parmesan cheese (30g)
- Salt and pepper to taste
- Vegetable oil for frying
- For the Caesar Salad:
- 4 cups fresh Romaine lettuce, torn into bite-sized pieces (120g)
- 1/4 cup Caesar salad dressing (60g)
- 1/4 cup grated Parmesan cheese (30g)
- Croutons for garnish (optional)

1. In one bowl, place all-purpose flour. In another bowl, add the beaten eggs. In a third bowl, mix the panko breadcrumbs, grated Parmesan cheese, salt, and pepper.
2. Dip each Brussels sprout half into the flour, then the beaten eggs, and finally coat it with the breadcrumb mixture.
3. Preheat your deep fryer or a large, deep skillet with vegetable oil to 350°F (175°C).
4. Carefully place the coated Brussels sprouts into the hot oil and fry for about 2-3 minutes or until they are golden brown and crispy. Remove with a slotted spoon and place on paper towels to drain excess oil.
5. In a large bowl, combine the Romaine lettuce and Caesar salad dressing. Toss to coat the lettuce with the dressing.
6. Top the salad with the Crispy Fried Brussels Sprouts, grated Parmesan cheese, and croutons if desired.

Fried Avocado Tacos with Cilantro Lime Sauce

Serves 2 / Prep Time: 15 minutes / Cook Time: 15 minutes

- For the Fried Avocado Tacos:
- 2 ripe avocados, sliced into wedges (200g each)
- 100g all-purpose flour
- 2 large eggs
- 150g panko breadcrumbs
- 1 teaspoon paprika
- 1 teaspoon garlic powder
- Salt and pepper to taste

- Vegetable oil for frying
- For the Cilantro Lime Sauce:
- 1/2 cup mayonnaise (115g)
- 1/4 cup sour cream (60g)
- 2 tablespoons fresh lime juice
- 2 tablespoons chopped fresh cilantro
- 1 clove garlic, minced
- Salt and pepper to taste
- For Assembling Tacos:
- 4 small flour tortillas
- 1 cup shredded lettuce (50g)
- 1/2 cup diced tomatoes (100g)
- 1/4 cup diced red onion (50g)

1. Start by preparing the Cilantro Lime Sauce. In a bowl, combine mayonnaise, sour cream, fresh lime juice, chopped cilantro, minced garlic, salt, and pepper. Mix well, then refrigerate the sauce while you prepare the rest of the dish.
2. Heat the Ninja Dual Zone Air Fryer to 350°F (175°C).
3. While the Air Fryer heats up, prepare the avocado wedges. In three separate bowls, place the all-purpose flour in one, whisk the eggs in another, and mix the panko breadcrumbs with paprika, garlic powder, salt, and pepper in the third.
4. Take each avocado wedge and dip it in the flour, then the egg, and finally coat it in the breadcrumb mixture. Set them aside on a plate.
5. Carefully place the breaded avocado wedges into the hot Air Fryer and air fry until golden brown, about 2-3 minutes per side. Remove with a slotted spoon and place on paper towels.
6. Warm up the tortilla in the second zone of the air fryer.
7. Place a generous spoonful of the Cilantro Lime Sauce on each tortilla.
8. Add the crispy fried avocado wedges.
9. Top with shredded lettuce, diced tomatoes, and red onion.
10. Serve immediately and enjoy!

Crispy Fried Zucchini Blossoms Stuffed with Goat Cheese

Serves 2 / Prep Time: 15 minutes / Cook Time: 10 minutes

- 4 fresh zucchini blossoms
- 100g goat cheese
- 50g all-purpose flour
- 1 egg, beaten
- 50g breadcrumbs
- 1/2 teaspoon dried oregano
- Salt and pepper to taste
- Vegetable oil for frying

1. Carefully remove the stamen from inside each zucchini blossom and gently rinse them under cold water. Pat them dry with a paper towel.
2. Gently stuff each blossom with goat cheese, being careful not to overfill.
3. In three separate bowls, place the all-purpose flour in one, the beaten egg in another, and mix the breadcrumbs with dried oregano, salt, and pepper in the third.
4. Dip each stuffed zucchini blossom into the flour, then the beaten egg, and finally coat them in the breadcrumb mixture. Set them aside on a plate.
5. In a deep fryer or a large, deep skillet, heat vegetable oil to 350°F (175°C).
6. Carefully place the breaded zucchini blossoms into the hot oil and fry for about 2-3 minutes or until they are golden brown and crispy. Remove with a slotted spoon and place on paper towels to drain excess oil.

Buffalo Cauliflower Wraps

Serves 2 / Prep Time: 20 minutes / Cook Time: 20 minutes

- For the Buffalo Cauliflower:
- 300g cauliflower florets
- 30g all-purpose flour
- 5g garlic powder
- 5g onion powder
- 5g salt
- 5g black pepper
- 1 egg
- 30g hot sauce
- For the Wrap Assembly:
- 4 large whole wheat tortillas
- 60g shredded lettuce
- 60g diced tomatoes
- 60g diced celery
- 60g crumbled blue cheese
- 30g ranch dressing

1. In a bowl, combine the all-purpose flour, garlic powder, onion powder, salt, and black pepper for the cauliflower coating.
2. In another bowl, whisk together the egg and hot sauce. Dip each cauliflower floret into the egg mixture, then into the flour mixture, ensuring they are well-coated.
3. Preheat your Ninja Foodi Dual Zone Air Fryer to 375°F (190°C) using the "Air Fry" setting.
4. Lightly grease the air fryer basket with cooking oil.
5. Place the coated cauliflower in the air fryer basket.

6. Air fry for about 15-20 minutes or until the cauliflower is crispy and cooked through.
7. While the cauliflower is cooking, prepare the wrap ingredients. Place shredded lettuce, diced tomatoes, diced celery, crumbled blue cheese, and ranch dressing in separate bowls.
8. Once the cauliflower is done, assemble the wraps by placing a portion of the cauliflower and the other prepared ingredients in each tortilla.

Crispy Fried Asparagus

Serves 2 / Prep Time: 15 minutes / Cook Time: 10 minutes

- 200g fresh asparagus spears
- 50g all-purpose flour
- 5g garlic powder
- 5g onion powder
- 5g salt
- 5g black pepper
- 1 egg
- Cooking oil, for frying

1. In a bowl, combine the all-purpose flour, garlic powder, onion powder, salt, and black pepper.
2. In another bowl, beat the egg. Dip each asparagus spear into the egg, then into the flour mixture, ensuring they are well-coated.
3. Preheat your Ninja Foodi Dual Zone Air Fryer to 375°F (190°C) using the "Air Fry" setting.
4. Lightly grease the air fryer basket with cooking oil.
5. Place the coated asparagus spears in the air fryer basket.
6. Air fry for about 8-10 minutes or until the asparagus is crispy and tender.

Crispy Fried Tofu

Serves 2 / Prep Time: 15 minutes / Cook Time: 20 minutes

- 300g extra-firm tofu, pressed and cubed
- 30g cornstarch
- 15g soy sauce
- 5g garlic powder
- 5g paprika
- 2g salt
- 2g black pepper
- Cooking spray

1. Press the tofu to remove excess moisture and cut it into bite-sized cubes.
2. Toss the tofu cubes in cornstarch until they are evenly coated.
3. In a separate bowl, combine soy sauce, garlic powder, paprika, salt, and black pepper. Toss the cornstarch-coated tofu in this mixture to season.
4. Preheat your Ninja Foodi Dual Zone Air Fryer to 375°F (190°C) for 5 minutes.
5. Place the seasoned tofu cubes in the air fryer basket, making sure they are not overcrowded.
6. Air fry for 15-20 minutes or until the tofu is crispy and golden brown, shaking or flipping the tofu halfway through for even cooking.
7. Remove the crispy fried tofu from the air fryer and serve hot with your favorite dipping sauce.

Garlic Herb Roasted Chickpeas

Serves 2 / Prep Time: 10 minutes / Cook Time: 20 minutes

- 200g canned chickpeas, drained and rinsed
- 10g olive oil
- 5g minced garlic
- 2g dried rosemary
- 2g dried thyme
- 2g dried oregano
- Salt and black pepper to taste

1. Preheat your Ninja Foodi Dual Zone Air Fryer to 375°F (190°C) using the "Air Fry" setting.
2. In a bowl, combine the chickpeas, olive oil, minced garlic, dried rosemary, dried thyme, dried oregano, salt, and black pepper. Toss to coat the chickpeas evenly.
3. Place the seasoned chickpeas in the air fryer basket in a single layer.
4. Air fry the chickpeas for about 15-20 minutes, shaking the basket or tossing the chickpeas halfway through to ensure even cooking. They should become crispy and golden.
5. Remove the chickpeas from the air fryer and let them cool slightly before serving.

Air Fryer Vegetarian Spring Rolls

Serves 2 / Prep Time: 20 minutes / Cook Time: 10 minutes

- 100g vermicelli rice noodles
- 8 spring roll wrappers
- 100g tofu, sliced into strips
- 50g cucumber, julienned
- 50g carrot, julienned
- 50g bell pepper, julienned
- 20g fresh mint leaves
- 20g fresh cilantro leaves
- 10g toasted sesame seeds
- 10g hoisin sauce (for dipping)
- 5g soy sauce (for dipping)

1. Preheat your Ninja Foodi Dual Zone Air Fryer to

375°F (190°C) on the "Air Fry" setting.
2. Cook the vermicelli rice noodles according to package instructions, drain, and set aside.
3. In one air fryer zone, arrange the tofu slices and air fry at 375°F (190°C) for about 8-10 minutes, or until they are crispy.
4. In the other zone, place a damp paper towel on a clean surface. Soak a spring roll wrapper in warm water for about 20 seconds until it becomes pliable, then lay it on the damp paper towel.
5. Layer the tofu, cucumber, carrot, bell pepper, mint leaves, cilantro leaves, and vermicelli noodles on the wrapper.
6. Fold the sides in and roll up the wrapper, sealing the edges.
7. Repeat with the remaining wrappers and ingredients.
8. Air fry the vegetarian spring rolls at 375°F (190°C) for about 8-10 minutes, or until they are crispy and golden.
9. Serve your Vegetarian Spring Rolls hot with hoisin and soy sauce for dipping.
10. Enjoy this light and delicious appetizer or snack!

Air Fryer Ratatouille Quiche

Serves 2 / Prep Time: 20 minutes / Cook Time: 25 minutes

- For the Quiche Filling:
- 100g zucchini, diced
- 100g eggplant, diced
- 100g red bell pepper, diced
- 100g yellow onion, diced
- 10g olive oil
- 5g garlic, minced
- 4 eggs
- 100ml milk
- 50g grated Parmesan cheese
- 5g fresh basil, chopped
- Salt and black pepper to taste
- For the Crust:

1. 2 sheets of puff pastry, thawed
2. Preheat your Ninja Foodi Dual Zone Air Fryer to 375°F (190°C) on the "Air Fry" setting.
3. In a bowl, toss the diced zucchini, eggplant, red bell pepper, and yellow onion with olive oil and minced garlic.
4. In another bowl, beat the eggs and mix them with milk, grated Parmesan cheese, chopped fresh basil, salt, and black pepper.
5. Cut one sheet of puff pastry into a circle that will fit in your air fryer zone. This will be the bottom crust.
6. Cut the other sheet into strips to form the sides of the quiche.
7. In one air fryer zone, place the bottom puff pastry circle.
8. Air fry at 375°F (190°C) for about 5-7 minutes, or until it is golden brown.
9. In the other air fryer zone, place the diced vegetables.
10. Air fry at 375°F (190°C) for about 10 minutes, or until they are tender and slightly browned.
11. Pour the egg and cheese mixture over the bottom crust.
12. Arrange the air-fried vegetables on top.
13. Place the puff pastry strips around the edges to create the sides of the quiche.
14. Air fry the quiche at 375°F (190°C) for about 10-15 minutes, or until it's set and golden.
15. Serve your Air Fryer Ratatouille Quiche!

Fried Mozzarella Caprese Salad

Serves 2 / Prep Time: 15 minutes / Cook Time: 10 minutes

- 200g fresh mozzarella cheese, cut into cubes
- 50g all-purpose flour
- 2 eggs, beaten
- 100g breadcrumbs
- Cooking spray
- 100g cherry tomatoes
- Fresh basil leaves
- Balsamic glaze for drizzling

1. Dredge the mozzarella cubes in flour, then dip them in beaten eggs, and finally coat with breadcrumbs.
2. Preheat your Ninja Foodi Dual Zone Air Fryer to 375°F (190°C).
3. Place the breaded mozzarella cubes in the air fryer basket, making sure they are not touching.
4. Air fry at 375°F (190°C) for 5-7 minutes or until they are golden brown and crispy.
5. Arrange the fried mozzarella cubes on a plate with cherry tomatoes and fresh basil leaves.
6. Drizzle with balsamic glaze.

Crispy Fried Green Bean and Mushroom Stir-Fry

Serves 2 / Prep Time: 20 minutes / Cook Time: 15 minutes

- 200g green beans, trimmed and cut into bite-sized pieces
- 150g mushrooms, sliced
- 50g all-purpose flour
- 2 eggs, beaten

- 100g breadcrumbs
- Cooking spray
- 50g soy sauce
- 10g oyster sauce
- 10g honey
- 5g minced garlic
- 5g minced ginger
- 5g sesame oil

1. Dredge the green beans and mushroom slices in flour, dip them in beaten eggs, and coat with breadcrumbs.
2. Preheat your Ninja Foodi Dual Zone Air Fryer to 375°F (190°C).
3. Place the breaded green beans and mushrooms in the air fryer basket, ensuring they are not touching.
4. Air fry at 375°F (190°C) for 10-12 minutes or until they are crispy and golden brown.
5. In a small saucepan, combine soy sauce, oyster sauce, honey, minced garlic, minced ginger, and sesame oil. Heat over low heat, stirring until the sauce thickens.
6. Toss the air-fried green beans and mushrooms in the stir-fry sauce until well coated.

Crispy Fried Avocado and Black Bean Tacos with Lime Crema

Serves 2 / Prep Time: 25 minutes / Cook Time: 15 minutes

- 2 ripe avocados, sliced
- 200g black beans, drained and rinsed
- 100g cornmeal
- 100g all-purpose flour
- 1 tsp chili powder
- 1/2 tsp cumin
- 1/2 tsp salt
- 1/4 tsp black pepper
- 2 eggs, beaten
- Cooking spray
- 4 small corn tortillas
- For Lime Crema:
- 100g Greek yogurt
- Juice of 1 lime
- 1/2 tsp garlic powder
- Salt and pepper to taste

1. In one bowl, combine cornmeal, flour, chili powder, cumin, salt, and pepper.
2. Dip avocado slices into the beaten eggs, then coat them with the cornmeal mixture.
3. Preheat your Ninja Foodi Dual Zone Air Fryer to 375°F (190°C).
4. Place the coated avocado slices in the air fryer basket. Spray with cooking spray.
5. Air fry at 375°F (190°C) for 8-10 minutes, or until they are crispy and golden brown.
6. While the avocados are frying, warm the black beans in a microwave or on the stovetop.
7. In a small bowl, whisk together the Greek yogurt, lime juice, garlic powder, salt, and pepper to make the lime crema.
8. Warm the corn tortillas in the air fryer for 2 minutes.
9. Spread a spoonful of black beans on each tortilla.
10. Place fried avocado slices on top of the beans.
11. Drizzle with lime crema.

Crispy Fried Zucchini Noodle Salad with Lemon Vinaigrette

Serves 2 / Prep Time: 15 minutes / Cook Time: 10 minutes

- For the Zucchini Noodles:
- 2 medium zucchinis, spiralized (about 200g each)
- 100g all-purpose flour
- 1 egg, beaten
- 30g Panko breadcrumbs
- 5g paprika
- Salt and black pepper to taste
- For the Lemon Vinaigrette:
- 30g olive oil
- 10g lemon juice
- 5g Dijon mustard
- 5g honey
- 5g fresh thyme, chopped
- Salt and black pepper to taste
- For the Salad:
- Mixed greens (about 100g)
- Cherry tomatoes (about 100g), halved
- Red onion (about 50g), thinly sliced
- Feta cheese (about 30g), crumbled

1. Preheat your Ninja Foodi Dual Zone Air Fryer to 375°F (190°C) on the "Air Fry" setting.
2. Spiralize the zucchini to create zucchini noodles.
3. In one bowl, place the all-purpose flour. In another, have the beaten egg ready. In a third bowl, mix Panko breadcrumbs, paprika, salt, and black pepper.
4. In a small jar, combine the olive oil, lemon juice, Dijon mustard, honey, chopped fresh thyme, salt, and black pepper to make the lemon vinaigrette.
5. In one air fryer zone, coat the zucchini noodles in flour, then dip them in the beaten egg, and finally coat them in the breadcrumb mixture.
6. Place the coated zucchini noodles in the air fryer

basket.
7. Air fry at 375°F (190°C) for about 8-10 minutes, turning them once or twice during cooking, until they are crispy and golden.
8. In the other air fryer zone, place the cherry tomatoes and red onion slices.
9. Air fry for about 2-3 minutes, or until the vegetables are slightly softened and caramelized.
10. On a serving platter, arrange the mixed greens, followed by the crispy zucchini noodles.
11. Top with the air-fried cherry tomatoes, red onion, and crumbled feta cheese.
12. Drizzle the lemon vinaigrette over the salad.
13. Serve your Crispy Fried Zucchini Noodle Salad with Lemon Vinaigrette.

Air Fryer Ratatouille

Serves 2 / Prep Time: 20 minutes / Cook Time: 20 minutes

- 1 small eggplant (about 300g), diced
- 2 small zucchinis (about 200g), diced
- 1 red bell pepper (about 150g), diced
- 1 yellow bell pepper (about 150g), diced
- 1 red onion (about 150g), diced
- 3 cloves garlic, minced
- 100g canned crushed tomatoes
- 10g olive oil
- 5g dried thyme
- 5g dried oregano
- Salt and black pepper to taste
- Fresh basil leaves for garnish

1. Preheat your Ninja Foodi Dual Zone Air Fryer to 375°F (190°C) on the "Air Fry" setting.
2. In a large bowl, combine the diced eggplant, zucchinis, red and yellow bell peppers, red onion, minced garlic, crushed tomatoes, olive oil, dried thyme, dried oregano, salt, and black pepper. Toss to coat the vegetables evenly.
3. Divide the vegetable mixture between the two air fryer zones.
4. Air fry at 375°F (190°C) for about 18-20 minutes, tossing the vegetables once or twice during cooking, until they are tender and slightly caramelized.
5. Garnish with fresh basil leaves before serving.
6. Serve your Ratatouille hot as a delicious side dish or as a main course.

Air Fryer Stuffed Acorn Squash with Quinoa and Cranberries

Serves 2 / Prep Time: 20 minutes / Cook Time: 30 minutes

- 1 acorn squash
- 100g quinoa, cooked
- 40g dried cranberries
- 30g chopped pecans
- 10g olive oil
- 5g maple syrup
- 2. 5g ground cinnamon
- Salt and black pepper to taste

1. Preheat your Ninja Foodi Dual Zone Air Fryer to 375°F (190°C) on the "Air Fry" setting.
2. Cut the acorn squash in half and remove the seeds.
3. In a bowl, mix the cooked quinoa, dried cranberries, chopped pecans, olive oil, maple syrup, ground cinnamon, salt, and black pepper.
4. Stuff the acorn squash halves with the quinoa and cranberry mixture.
5. Place the stuffed acorn squash halves in the air fryer basket.
6. Air fry at 375°F (190°C) for about 30 minutes, or until the squash is tender and the filling is heated through.
7. Serve your Stuffed Acorn Squash with Quinoa and Cranberries hot, and enjoy this flavorful dish.

Air Fryer Cabbage Steaks

Serves 2 / Prep Time: 10 minutes / Cook Time: 15 minutes

- 400g cabbage
- 30g olive oil
- 5g garlic powder
- 5g onion powder
- 5g paprika
- Salt and black pepper to taste

1. Start by prepping the cabbage. Cut it into 1-inch thick slices, making "steaks."
2. In a small bowl, mix the olive oil, garlic powder, onion powder, paprika, salt, and black pepper.
3. Brush both sides of the cabbage steaks with the olive oil mixture.
4. Preheat your Ninja Foodi Dual Zone Air Fryer to 375°F (190°C) on the "Air Fry" setting.
5. Place the cabbage steaks into the air fryer basket, making sure they don't overlap.
6. Air fry the cabbage steaks at 375°F (190°C) for about 15 minutes, flipping them over halfway through the cooking time. The steaks should be tender and slightly crispy on the outside.
7. Once done, remove the cabbage steaks from the air fryer and serve immediately.

Air Fryer Green Bean Fries

Serves 2 / Prep Time: 10 minutes / Cook Time: 10 minutes

- 200g fresh green beans, ends trimmed
- 10g olive oil
- 5g grated Parmesan cheese
- 5g breadcrumbs
- 2. 5g garlic powder
- Salt and black pepper to taste

1. Preheat your Ninja Foodi Dual Zone Air Fryer to 375°F (190°C) on the "Air Fry" setting.
2. In a bowl, toss the trimmed green beans with olive oil, garlic powder, salt, and black pepper until they are well-coated.
3. In a separate bowl, combine the grated Parmesan cheese and breadcrumbs.
4. Dredge each green bean in the Parmesan and breadcrumb mixture, making sure they are evenly coated.
5. Place the coated green beans in the air fryer basket. Make sure they are in a single layer and not crowded.
6. Air fry at 375°F (190°C) for about 10 minutes, shaking the basket halfway through, until the green bean fries are crispy and golden brown.
7. Serve immediately and enjoy your air fryer green bean fries.

Green Beans with Garlic

Serves: 4 / Prep time: 10 minutes / Cook time: 12 minutes

- 300g green beans, trimmed
- 2 tbsp olive oil
- 2 cloves garlic, minced
- Salt and black pepper, to taste

1. Preheat the Ninja Dual Zone Air Fryer to 200°C on zone 1 for 5 minutes.
2. In a bowl, combine the green beans, olive oil, minced garlic, salt, and black pepper. Toss until the green beans are evenly coated.
3. Place the seasoned green beans in zone 1 of the air fryer.
4. Cook the green beans at 200°C for 12 minutes, shaking the basket halfway through the cooking time, or until they are tender-crisp and lightly browned.
5. Once cooked, remove the green beans from the air fryer and let them cool for a few minutes before serving.
6. Serve the green beans as a healthy and flavorful side dish. Enjoy the vibrant green colour and the aromatic garlic-infused taste!

Eggplant Fries

Serves: 4 / Prep time: 15 minutes / Cook time: 15 minutes

- 1 large eggplant
- 60g all-purpose flour
- 2 large eggs, beaten
- 120g breadcrumbs
- 1 tsp dried oregano
- 1/2 tsp garlic powder
- Salt and black pepper, to taste
- Olive oil spray

1. Preheat the Ninja Dual Zone Air Fryer to 200°C on zone 1 for 5 minutes.
2. Cut the eggplant into fry-shaped sticks.
3. Place the flour in a shallow dish. In another dish, beat the eggs. In a third dish, combine the breadcrumbs, dried oregano, garlic powder, salt, and black pepper.
4. Dip each eggplant stick into the flour, then into the beaten eggs, and finally coat it with the breadcrumb mixture. Press the breadcrumbs onto the eggplant to ensure a good coating.
5. Place the coated eggplant fries in zone 1 of the air fryer. Spray them with olive oil spray to promote browning.
6. Cook the eggplant fries at 200°C for 15 minutes, flipping them halfway through the cooking time, or until they are crispy and golden brown.
7. Once cooked, remove the eggplant fries from the air fryer and let them cool for a few minutes before serving.
8. Serve the eggplant fries as a delicious and healthier alternative to traditional fries. Enjoy the crispy texture and the delicate flavour of the eggplant!

Roasted Carrot Fries

Serves: 4 / Prep time: 10 minutes / Cook time: 18 minutes

- 500g carrots, peeled and cut into fries
- 2 tbsp olive oil
- 1 tsp ground cumin
- 1/2 tsp paprika
- Salt and black pepper, to taste

1. Preheat the Ninja Dual Zone Air Fryer to 200°C on zone 1 for 5 minutes.
2. In a bowl, toss the carrot fries with olive oil, ground cumin, paprika, salt, and black pepper until well

coated.
3. Place the seasoned carrot fries in zone 1 of the air fryer.
4. Cook the fries at 200°C for 18 minutes, shaking the basket halfway through the cooking time, or until they are crispy and golden brown.
5. Once cooked, remove the carrot fries from the air fryer and let them cool for a few minutes before serving.
6. Serve the roasted carrot fries as a healthy and flavorful alternative to traditional fries. Enjoy the natural sweetness and the satisfying crunch!

Broiled Asparagus with Lemon and Parmesan

Serves: 4 / Prep time: 5 minutes / Cook time: 10 minutes

- 500g asparagus, tough ends removed
- 2 tbsp olive oil
- 1/2 tsp sea salt
- 1/4 tsp black pepper
- 1 lemon, zested and juiced
- 30g grated Parmesan cheese

1. Preheat the Ninja Dual Zone Air Fryer on Broil mode at 200°C.
2. Toss asparagus with olive oil, salt, and black pepper in a mixing bowl.
3. Arrange the asparagus in a single layer on the crisper plate and broil for 5-7 minutes until lightly charred and tender, shaking the basket once halfway through.
4. Transfer the asparagus to a serving platter and sprinkle with lemon zest, lemon juice, and Parmesan cheese.
5. Serve immediately and enjoy!

Dehydrated Vegetable Chips with Sea Salt

Serves: 4 / Prep time: 10 minutes / Cook time: 2-3 hours

- 2 large sweet potatoes
- 2 large carrots
- 2 large beets
- 1 tbsp olive oil
- 1 tsp sea salt

1. Preheat the Ninja Dual Zone Air Fryer on Dehydrate mode at 70°C.
2. Peel and thinly slice the vegetables using a mandolin or a sharp knife.
3. Toss the vegetables with olive oil and sea salt in a mixing bowl.
4. Arrange the vegetable slices in a single layer on the dehydrator rack, making sure to leave enough space between each slice for air circulation.
5. Dehydrate the vegetables for 2-3 hours, or until they are completely dried and crispy.
6. Transfer the vegetable chips to a bowl and serve!

Broiled Eggplant with Garlic and Tahini Sauce

Serves: 4 / Prep time: 15 minutes / Cook time: 15 minutes

- 1 large eggplant, sliced into rounds
- 1 tbsp olive oil
- Sea salt and black pepper, to taste
- 2 cloves garlic, minced
- 2 tbsp tahini
- 2 tbsp lemon juice
- 60ml water
- 1 tbsp chopped fresh parsley, for garnish

1. Preheat the Ninja Dual Zone Air Fryer to broil at 220°C.
2. Brush eggplant slices with olive oil and season with salt and pepper.
3. Arrange the eggplant slices in a single layer on the crisper plate.
4. Broil in zone 1 for 8 minutes.
5. While the eggplant is cooking, make the garlic and tahini sauce: In a small bowl, whisk together minced garlic, tahini, lemon juice, and water until smooth.
6. Remove the eggplant from the air fryer and arrange on a serving platter.
7. Drizzle the garlic and tahini sauce over the eggplant.
8. Garnish with chopped parsley and serve immediately.

chapter 8 Snacks

Air Fryer BBQ Ribs

Serves 2 / Prep Time: 15 minutes / Cook Time: 40 minutes

- 500g baby back ribs
- 1/4 cup BBQ sauce (60g)
- 1 tablespoon olive oil
- 1 teaspoon smoked paprika
- 1 teaspoon garlic powder
- 1/2 teaspoon salt
- 1/4 teaspoon black pepper

1. Start by removing the membrane from the back of the baby back ribs. This will help the seasonings penetrate the meat better.
2. In a bowl, mix together the olive oil, smoked paprika, garlic powder, salt, and black pepper to create a seasoning mixture.
3. Rub the seasoning mixture over both sides of the ribs.
4. Preheat your air fryer to 375°F (190°C).
5. Place the seasoned ribs in the air fryer basket.
6. Air fry the ribs at 375°F (190°C) for about 20 minutes on one side.
7. After 20 minutes, flip the ribs, baste them with BBQ sauce, and air fry for an additional 20 minutes.
8. Make sure the ribs are cooked through and have a nice char on the outside.

Air Fryer Honey Mustard Chicken Tenders

Serves 2 / Prep Time: 15 minutes / Cook Time: 15 minutes

- For the Honey Mustard Chicken Tenders:
- 400g chicken tenders
- 1/2 cup all-purpose flour (60g)
- 2 large eggs, beaten
- 1 cup panko breadcrumbs (120g)
- 1/4 cup honey mustard sauce (60g)
- 1/2 teaspoon garlic powder
- Salt and pepper to taste

1. In one bowl, place the all-purpose flour. In another bowl, add the beaten eggs. In a third bowl, mix the panko breadcrumbs, garlic powder, salt, and pepper.
2. Dip each chicken tender into the flour, then the beaten egg, and finally coat it with the breadcrumb mixture.
3. Preheat your air fryer to 375°F (190°C).
4. Place the coated chicken tenders in the air fryer basket in a single layer. You may need to cook them in batches if they don't all fit without crowding.
5. Air fry the tenders at 375°F (190°C) for about 12-15 minutes, turning them halfway through, until they are golden brown and cooked through.

Fried Chicken and Waffle Skewers with Maple Sriracha Glaze

Serves 2 / Prep Time: 20 minutes / Cook Time: 15 minutes

- For the Chicken and Waffle Skewers:
- 2 boneless, skinless chicken breasts, cut into cubes (300g)
- 1 cup all-purpose flour (120g)
- 2 large eggs, beaten
- 1 cup panko breadcrumbs (120g)
- 1/2 teaspoon salt
- 1/4 teaspoon black pepper
- 4 small frozen waffles
- Wooden skewers
- For the Maple Sriracha Glaze:
- 1/4 cup maple syrup (60g)
- 1 tablespoon Sriracha sauce
- 1/2 teaspoon soy sauce

1. In one bowl, place the all-purpose flour. In another bowl, add the beaten eggs. In a third bowl, fill it with panko breadcrumbs, salt, and black pepper.
2. Thread the chicken cubes onto wooden skewers.
3. Preheat your Ninja Foodi Dual Zone Air Fryer to 375°F (190°C).
4. Dip the chicken skewers into the flour, then the beaten eggs, and finally coat them with the breadcrumb mixture.
5. Place the chicken skewers in the air fryer basket.
6. Air fry at 375°F (190°C) for about 10-12 minutes, turning them halfway through, until the chicken is cooked through and the coating is crispy.
7. In the last few minutes of cooking, add the frozen waffles to the air fryer to warm them.
8. In a small saucepan, combine maple syrup, Sriracha sauce, and soy sauce. Heat over low heat until the mixture is well combined and slightly thickened.
9. Serve the Chicken and Waffle Skewers with the

warm maple Sriracha glaze for drizzling.

Fried Cheeseburger Egg Rolls

Serves 2 / Prep Time: 20 minutes / Cook Time: 10 minutes

- 4 egg roll wrappers
- 200g ground beef
- 1/2 cup shredded cheddar cheese (60g)
- 1/4 cup diced onion (30g)
- 1/4 cup diced pickles (30g)
- 2 tablespoons ketchup
- 2 tablespoons yellow mustard
- Vegetable oil for frying

1. In a skillet, cook the ground beef over medium heat until browned. Drain any excess fat.
2. In a bowl, mix the cooked ground beef with diced onion, diced pickles, ketchup, and yellow mustard.
3. Lay out an egg roll wrapper with one corner pointing towards you. Place a portion of the beef mixture and a sprinkle of cheddar cheese on the wrapper.
4. Fold the sides of the wrapper in towards the center, then roll it up tightly, sealing the top corner with a bit of water to make a secure seal.
5. Repeat this process for the remaining wrappers and filling.
6. Preheat your Ninja Foodi Dual Zone Air Fryer to 375°F (190°C).
7. Brush or spray the egg rolls with a little vegetable oil to help them crisp up in the air fryer.
8. Place the egg rolls in the air fryer basket.
9. Cook at 375°F (190°C) for about 10 minutes, turning halfway through, or until they are golden brown and crispy.

Crispy Fried Coconut Tofu with Sweet Chili Sauce

Serves 2 / Prep Time: 15 minutes / Cook Time: 15 minutes

- For the Crispy Fried Coconut Tofu:
- 200g firm tofu, cut into cubes
- 1/2 cup shredded unsweetened coconut (40g)
- 1/4 cup all-purpose flour (30g)
- 1/4 cup cornstarch (30g)
- 1 teaspoon salt
- 1/2 teaspoon black pepper
- 1/2 cup unsweetened coconut milk (120g)
- Vegetable oil for frying
- For the Sweet Chili Sauce:
- 1/4 cup sweet chili sauce (60g)
- 1 tablespoon rice vinegar
- 1 tablespoon soy sauce
- 1 teaspoon minced garlic

1. Start by preparing the Sweet Chili Sauce. In a small bowl, combine sweet chili sauce, rice vinegar, soy sauce, and minced garlic. Mix well and set aside.
2. In one bowl, combine the shredded coconut, all-purpose flour, cornstarch, salt, and black pepper. In another bowl, pour the unsweetened coconut milk.
3. Dip each tofu cube into the coconut milk, allowing excess to drip off, and then coat it with the coconut-flour mixture. Ensure each tofu cube is well-coated.
4. Preheat your air fryer to 350°F (175°C).
5. Carefully place the coated tofu cubes into the airfryer and fry for about 3-4 minutes or until they are golden brown and crispy. Remove with a slotted spoon and place on paper towels.
6. Serve the Crispy Fried Coconut Tofu with the Sweet Chili Sauce for dipping.

Buffalo Chicken Sliders

Serves 2 / Prep Time: 20 minutes / Cook Time: 15 minutes

- For the Buffalo Chicken:
- 300g boneless, skinless chicken breasts
- 30g hot sauce
- 15g butter, melted
- 5g garlic powder
- 5g onion powder
- 5g salt
- 5g black pepper
- For the Sliders:
- 4 small slider buns
- 60g blue cheese dressing
- 60g shredded lettuce
- 60g sliced tomatoes
- 60g red onion, thinly sliced
- Cooking oil, for brushing

1. Preheat your Ninja Foodi Dual Zone Air Fryer to 375°F (190°C) using the "Air Fry" setting.
2. In a bowl, combine hot sauce, melted butter, garlic powder, onion powder, salt, and black pepper to make the buffalo sauce.
3. Cut the chicken breasts into slider-sized pieces and toss them in the buffalo sauce.
4. Lightly brush the air fryer basket with cooking oil.
5. Place the buffalo chicken pieces in the air fryer basket.
6. Air fry for about 12-15 minutes or until the chicken is cooked through and crispy.
7. While the chicken is cooking, prepare the sliders by

spreading blue cheese dressing on each bun. Add shredded lettuce, sliced tomatoes, and red onion.
8. Once the chicken is done, place a piece of buffalo chicken on each slider bun, and assemble the sliders.

Air Fryer Apple Chips

Serves 2 / Prep Time: 10 minutes / Cook Time: 15 minutes

- 2 large apples, cored and sliced thinly
- 5g ground cinnamon
- 5g sugar (optional)
- Cooking oil spray

1. Preheat your Ninja Foodi Dual Zone Air Fryer to 350°F (175°C) using the "Air Fry" setting.
2. In a bowl, toss the apple slices with ground cinnamon and sugar if desired.
3. Lightly grease the air fryer basket with cooking oil spray.
4. Place the seasoned apple slices in a single layer in the air fryer basket. You may need to cook them in batches.
5. Air fry for about 12-15 minutes, flipping the apple slices halfway through, until they are crisp and lightly browned.
6. Remove the apple chips from the air fryer and let them cool before serving.

Fried Mozzarella Balls

Serves 2 / Prep Time: 20 minutes / Cook Time: 10 minutes

- 200g fresh mozzarella balls (small)
- 50g all-purpose flour
- 2g salt
- 2g black pepper
- 1 egg
- 30g breadcrumbs
- 30g grated Parmesan cheese
- Cooking oil, for frying

1. In one bowl, combine flour, salt, and black pepper. In another bowl, beat the egg.
2. In a third bowl, mix breadcrumbs and grated Parmesan cheese.
3. Dredge each mozzarella ball in the flour mixture, then dip it in the beaten egg, and finally coat it with the breadcrumb mixture, pressing the breadcrumbs onto the mozzarella ball to adhere.
4. Preheat your air fryer to 375°F (190°C) using the "Air Fry" setting.
5. Lightly grease the air fryer basket with cooking oil.
6. Place the breaded mozzarella balls in the air fryer basket.
7. Air fry for about 8-10 minutes or until the mozzarella balls are golden and have started to melt.
8. Remove from the air fryer and let them cool slightly before serving.

Crispy Fried Onion Strings

Serves 2 / Prep Time: 15 minutes / Cook Time: 10 minutes

- 100g thinly sliced onion rings
- 100g all-purpose flour
- 5g paprika
- 5g garlic powder
- 5g salt
- 2g black pepper
- 1 egg
- 30g buttermilk
- Cooking oil, for frying

1. In a bowl, mix together the flour, paprika, garlic powder, salt, and black pepper. This will be the dry coating.
2. In another bowl, beat the egg and mix in the buttermilk.
3. Heat cooking oil in a deep fryer or a heavy-bottomed pot to 350°F (175°C).
4. Dip the onion rings into the dry coating, then into the egg and buttermilk mixture, and back into the dry coating, ensuring they are well-coated.
5. Fry the coated onion strings in batches for about 2-3 minutes or until they are golden brown and crispy.
6. Remove the fried onion strings and drain them on a paper towel.

Egg Rolls

Serves 2 / Prep Time: 25 minutes / Cook Time: 15 minutes

- 100g ground pork
- 100g coleslaw mix (cabbage and carrots)
- 50g mushrooms, finely chopped
- 20g soy sauce
- 10g ginger, minced
- 5g garlic, minced
- 4 egg roll wrappers
- Cooking spray

1. In a skillet, brown the ground pork over medium heat. Add mushrooms, coleslaw mix, soy sauce, ginger, and garlic. Cook until the vegetables are

tender, and the mixture is well combined.
2. Lay out an egg roll wrapper with a corner pointing towards you. Place about 1/4 of the filling in the center.
3. Fold the corner closest to you over the filling, then fold in the sides and roll it up tightly.
4. Moisten the top corner with water to seal the edge of the wrapper.
5. Preheat your Ninja Foodi Dual Zone Air Fryer to 375°F (190°C) for 5 minutes.
6. Spray the egg rolls with cooking spray, then place them in the air fryer basket, making sure they are not touching.
7. Air fry for 12-15 minutes, flipping them halfway through, until they are golden and crispy.
8. Remove the egg rolls from the air fryer and serve with your favorite dipping sauce.

Chicken Satay Skewers

Serves 2 / Prep Time: 20 minutes / Cook Time: 10 minutes

- 300g boneless, skinless chicken breasts, cut into 1-inch cubes
- 60g peanut butter
- 15g soy sauce
- 15g honey
- 10g lime juice
- 10g minced garlic
- 5g minced ginger
- 5g curry powder
- 5g turmeric
- 2g cayenne pepper (adjust to taste)
- Salt and black pepper to taste
- For the Peanut Sauce:
- 40g peanut butter
- 20g coconut milk
- 10g soy sauce
- 5g honey
- 5g lime juice
- 2g minced garlic
- For Skewers:
- 4 wooden skewers, soaked in water for 30 minutes

1. In a bowl, mix together peanut butter, soy sauce, honey, lime juice, minced garlic, minced ginger, curry powder, turmeric, cayenne pepper, salt, and black pepper to make the chicken marinade.
2. Thread the chicken cubes onto the soaked skewers.
3. Place the chicken skewers in a shallow dish and pour the marinade over them. Ensure the chicken is well-coated. Marinate for at least 30 minutes, or overnight in the refrigerator.
4. Preheat your Ninja Foodi Dual Zone Air Fryer to 400°F (200°C) using the "Air Fry" setting.
5. Place the chicken skewers in the air fryer basket in a single layer. You may need to cook them in batches.
6. Cook for 5 minutes, then flip the skewers and cook for an additional 5 minutes or until the chicken is cooked through and has a slight char.
7. While the chicken is cooking, prepare the peanut sauce. In a small saucepan, combine peanut butter, coconut milk, soy sauce, honey, lime juice, and minced garlic. Heat over low heat, stirring until the sauce is smooth.
8. Serve the chicken satay skewers with the peanut sauce for dipping.

Air Fryer Kale Chips

Serves 2 / Prep Time: 10 minutes / Cook Time: 5 minutes

- 200g fresh kale, washed and dried
- 10g olive oil
- 5g nutritional yeast (optional)
- Salt and black pepper to taste

1. Remove the tough stems from the kale leaves and tear them into bite-sized pieces.
2. In a bowl, toss the kale with olive oil, nutritional yeast (if using), salt, and black pepper.
3. Preheat your Ninja Foodi Dual Zone Air Fryer to 375°F (190°C).
4. Place the kale in the air fryer basket in a single layer.
5. Air fry at 375°F (190°C) for 4-5 minutes, shaking the basket once halfway through. The kale should be crispy but not browned.

Air Fryer Mini Tacos

Serves 2 / Prep Time: 20 minutes / Cook Time: 10 minutes

- 150g ground beef
- 150g black beans, drained and rinsed
- 5g taco seasoning
- 50g shredded cheddar cheese
- 4 mini flour tortillas
- Cooking spray

1. Toppings of your choice (lettuce, tomatoes, salsa, sour cream, etc.)
2. In a skillet, brown the ground beef and add the taco seasoning. Stir in the black beans.
3. Preheat your Ninja Foodi Dual Zone Air Fryer to 375°F (190°C).
4. Lay out the mini tortillas and place the beef and black bean mixture on one half of each tortilla. Top

with shredded cheddar cheese.
5. Fold the tortillas in half to create semi-circles.
6. Spray the tacos with cooking spray and place them in the air fryer basket.
7. Air fry at 375°F (190°C) for 6-8 minutes or until they are crispy and the cheese is melted.

Air Fryer Donuts

Serves 2 / Prep Time: 20 minutes / Cook Time: 10 minutes

- 200g all-purpose flour
- 5g baking powder
- 50g sugar
- 5g salt
- 10g unsalted butter, melted
- 1 egg
- 100g milk
- Cooking spray
- 50g powdered sugar
- 10g milk
- 5g vanilla extract

1. In a mixing bowl, combine all-purpose flour, baking powder, sugar, and salt.
2. In another bowl, whisk together melted butter, egg, and milk.
3. Combine the wet and dry ingredients until a dough forms.
4. Roll out the dough on a floured surface and cut out donuts using a donut cutter.
5. In a separate bowl, mix powdered sugar, milk, and vanilla extract to create the glaze.
6. Preheat your Ninja Foodi Dual Zone Air Fryer to 350°F (175°C).
7. Spray the air fryer basket with cooking spray and place the donuts inside.
8. Air fry at 350°F (175°C) for 6-8 minutes or until the donuts are golden brown.
9. Dip the warm donuts into the glaze and let them set for a few minutes.

Molten Lava Cakes

Serves 2 / Prep Time: 15 minutes / Cook Time: 10 minutes

- 60g semi-sweet chocolate
- 30g unsalted butter
- 30g powdered sugar
- 20g all-purpose flour
- 2 eggs
- 5ml vanilla extract
- Pinch of salt
- Cocoa powder (for dusting)
- Fresh berries (optional, for garnish)

1. Preheat your Ninja Foodi Dual Zone Air Fryer to 375°F (190°C) on the "Bake/Roast" setting.
2. In a microwave-safe bowl, melt the chocolate and butter together in short intervals, stirring until smooth.
3. In another bowl, whisk the eggs, powdered sugar, vanilla extract, and a pinch of salt until well combined.
4. Gradually add the melted chocolate and butter mixture to the egg mixture, stirring until smooth.
5. Gently fold in the all-purpose flour until no lumps remain.
6. Grease two ramekins with butter and dust them with cocoa powder.
7. Pour the batter into the prepared ramekins.
8. In one air fryer zone, place the ramekins.
9. Air fry at 375°F (190°C) for about 8-10 minutes. The edges should be set, but the center should still be slightly soft.
10. In the other air fryer zone, place the ramekins.
11. Air fry for an additional 2 minutes.
12. Remove the lava cakes from the air fryer, let them cool for a minute, and then carefully invert them onto plates.
13. Serve your Molten Lava Cakes with fresh berries if desired.

Air Fryer Churro Bites

Serves 2 / Prep Time: 15 minutes / Cook Time: 15 minutes

- 150g all-purpose flour
- 30g unsalted butter
- 250ml water
- 5g granulated sugar
- 5g salt
- 5g ground cinnamon
- 1 egg
- 10ml vanilla extract
- 30g granulated sugar (for coating)
- 5g ground cinnamon (for coating)

1. Preheat your Ninja Foodi Dual Zone Air Fryer to 350°F (180°C) on the "Bake/Roast" setting.
2. In a saucepan, combine the water, butter, granulated sugar, and salt. Heat until the mixture comes to a boil.
3. Remove from heat and add the flour all at once, stirring until the mixture forms a ball.
4. Let the mixture cool for a few minutes.
5. In a bowl, whisk the egg and vanilla extract. Gradually add this mixture to the dough, stirring until smooth.

6. Transfer the dough to a piping bag with a star-shaped tip.
7. In one air fryer zone, pipe small churro bites onto a parchment-lined tray. p
8. Air fry at 350°F (180°C) for about 10-12 minutes or until they are golden brown.
9. In the other air fryer zone, mix the granulated sugar and ground cinnamon in a shallow dish.
10. Toss the hot churro bites in the cinnamon sugar mixture until well coated.
11. Serve your Air Fryer Churro Bites while they're still warm.

Mini Fruit Pies

Serves 2 / Prep Time: 20 minutes / Cook Time: 15 minutes

- 200g pie crust dough
- 150g mixed fresh fruit (e. g. , berries, apples, peaches)
- 30g granulated sugar
- 5g cornstarch
- 5ml lemon juice
- 5g ground cinnamon
- 10g unsalted butter
- 1 egg, beaten (for egg wash)
- 10g powdered sugar (for dusting)

1. Preheat your Ninja Foodi Dual Zone Air Fryer to 350°F (180°C) on the "Bake/Roast" setting.
2. In a bowl, combine the mixed fresh fruit, granulated sugar, cornstarch, lemon juice, and ground cinnamon. Stir until the fruit is coated.
3. Roll out the pie crust dough and cut it into four circles.
4. In one air fryer zone, place two of the pastry circles.
5. Spoon the fruit mixture onto the center of each pastry circle.
6. Dot each fruit pile with a small amount of unsalted butter.
7. Place the remaining pastry circles on top, creating mini pies. Seal the edges with a fork.
8. Brush the pies with beaten egg.
9. In the other air fryer zone, place the mini pies.
10. Air fry at 350°F (180°C) for about 12-15 minutes or until the pies are golden brown.
11. Let the Mini Fruit Pies cool slightly and dust them with powdered sugar.
12. Serve warm.

Corn Dogs

Serves 2 / Prep Time: 15 minutes / Cook Time: 15 minutes

- 2 hot dogs (approximately 100g each)
- 80g cornmeal
- 40g all-purpose flour
- 1/2 tsp baking powder
- 1/4 tsp salt
- 1/4 tsp black pepper
- 1 tbsp sugar
- 1 large egg
- 150ml buttermilk
- 2 bamboo skewers
- Cooking spray

1. Insert bamboo skewers into the center of each hot dog, leaving about 2 inches of the skewer exposed for a handle.
2. In a mixing bowl, combine the cornmeal, all-purpose flour, baking powder, salt, black pepper, and sugar.
3. In a separate bowl, whisk together the egg and buttermilk.
4. Dip each hot dog into the buttermilk mixture and then roll it in the dry mixture to coat it evenly. Repeat for a thicker coating.
5. Preheat the Ninja Foodi Dual Zone Air Fryer to 375°F (190°C) using the "Air Fry" setting.
6. Place the coated corn dogs in the Dual Zone Air Fryer basket, ensuring they are in a single layer and not overcrowded.
7. Spray the corn dogs lightly with cooking spray.
8. Set the Dual Zone Air Fryer to Air Fry at 375°F (190°C) for 12-15 minutes or until the corn dogs are golden brown and cooked through.
9. Serve hot with your favorite condiments.

Fried Ravioli

Serves 2 / Prep Time: 15 minutes / Cook Time: 15 minutes

- 200g fresh or frozen ravioli (cheese or meat-filled)
- 100g breadcrumbs
- 1/2 tsp Italian seasoning
- 1/4 tsp garlic powder
- 1/4 tsp salt
- 1/4 tsp black pepper
- 1 large egg, beaten
- Cooking spray
- Marinara sauce for dipping (optional)

1. In a bowl, combine breadcrumbs, Italian seasoning, garlic powder, salt, and black pepper.
2. Dip each ravioli into the beaten egg and then coat it with the breadcrumb mixture. Repeat for a thicker crust if desired.
3. Preheat the Ninja Foodi Dual Zone Air Fryer to

375°F (190°C) using the "Air Fry" setting.
4. Place the coated ravioli in the Dual Zone Air Fryer basket, ensuring they are in a single layer and not overcrowded.
5. Spray the ravioli with cooking spray.
6. Set the Dual Zone Air Fryer to Air Fry at 375°F (190°C) for 12-15 minutes or until the ravioli is crispy and golden brown.
7. Serve hot with marinara sauce for dipping, if desired.

Air Fryer Donut Twists

Serves 2 / Prep Time: 15 minutes / Cook Time: 10 minutes

- 200g refrigerated biscuit dough
- 30g granulated sugar
- 5g ground cinnamon
- 30g unsalted butter, melted
- 30g powdered sugar
- 5ml vanilla extract

1. Preheat your Ninja Foodi Dual Zone Air Fryer to 350°F (180°C) on the "Bake/Roast" setting.
2. In a shallow dish, combine the granulated sugar and ground cinnamon.
3. In another bowl, mix the melted butter, powdered sugar, and vanilla extract to make the glaze.
4. Roll out the biscuit dough into a rectangle.
5. In one air fryer zone, cut the dough into strips.
6. Twist each strip into a donut shape.
7. In the other air fryer zone, place the donut twists.
8. Air fry at 350°F (180°C) for about 8-10 minutes or until they are golden brown.
9. While the donut twists are still warm, roll them in the cinnamon sugar mixture.
10. Drizzle with the glaze.
11. Serve your Air Fryer Donut Twists while they're fresh and warm.

S'mores Crescent Rolls

Serves 2 / Prep Time: 15 minutes / Cook Time: 10 minutes

- 1 sheet of refrigerated crescent roll dough (about 200g)
- 20g milk chocolate chips
- 20g mini marshmallows
- 5g crushed graham crackers
- 10g unsalted butter, melted
- 5g powdered sugar

1. Preheat your Ninja Foodi Dual Zone Air Fryer to 350°F (180°C) on the "Bake/Roast" setting.
2. Unroll the crescent roll dough and separate it into triangles.
3. In a bowl, combine the milk chocolate chips, mini marshmallows, and crushed graham crackers.
4. In one air fryer zone, place a triangle of dough.
5. Spoon the chocolate, marshmallow, and graham cracker mixture onto the dough.
6. Roll up the crescent roll, sealing the edges.
7. In the other air fryer zone, place the crescent rolls.
8. Air fry at 350°F (180°C) for about 8-10 minutes or until they are golden brown and the marshmallows are gooey.
9. While the S'mores Crescent Rolls are still warm, brush them with melted butter and dust with powdered sugar.
10. Serve your S'mores Crescent Rolls warm.

Fried Cheese Curds

Serves 2 / Prep Time: 15 minutes / Cook Time: 10 minutes

- 150g cheese curds (preferably cold or frozen)
- 60g all-purpose flour
- 1/2 tsp salt
- 1/4 tsp black pepper
- 1 large egg
- 60ml milk
- 60g breadcrumbs
- Cooking spray
- Marinara sauce for dipping (optional)

1. In a bowl, combine all-purpose flour, salt, and black pepper.
2. In another bowl, whisk together the egg and milk to create an egg wash.
3. Dip each cheese curd into the flour mixture, then the egg wash, and finally into the breadcrumbs, coating them evenly. Repeat for a thicker coating.
4. Preheat the Ninja Foodi Dual Zone Air Fryer to 375°F (190°C) using the "Air Fry" setting.
5. Place the coated cheese curds in the Dual Zone Air Fryer basket, ensuring they are in a single layer and not overcrowded.
6. Spray the cheese curds lightly with cooking spray.
7. Set the Dual Zone Air Fryer to Air Fry at 375°F (190°C) for 8-10 minutes or until the cheese curds are crispy and golden brown.
8. Serve hot with marinara sauce for dipping, if desired.

Zeppoles (Italian Fried Dough Balls)

Serves 2 / Prep Time: 15 minutes / Cook Time: 10 minutes

- 150g all-purpose flour
- 20g granulated sugar

- 1/2 tsp salt
- 1/2 tsp baking powder
- 1/4 tsp vanilla extract
- 120ml warm milk
- 1 large egg
- Cooking spray
- Powdered sugar for dusting
- Optional: chocolate sauce or raspberry jam for dipping

1. In a mixing bowl, combine the all-purpose flour, granulated sugar, salt, and baking powder.
2. In a separate bowl, whisk together the warm milk, vanilla extract, and egg.
3. Pour the wet ingredients into the dry ingredients and stir until a sticky dough forms.
4. Preheat the Ninja Foodi Dual Zone Air Fryer to 375°F (190°C) using the "Air Fry" setting.
5. Using a cookie scoop or your hands, shape the dough into small, bite-sized balls, about 1 inch in diameter.
6. Place the dough balls in the Dual Zone Air Fryer basket, ensuring they are in a single layer and not overcrowded.
7. Spray the dough balls lightly with cooking spray.
8. Set the Dual Zone Air Fryer to Air Fry at 375°F (190°C) for 8-10 minutes or until the zeppoles are golden brown and cooked through. You may need to shake the basket or turn them halfway through for even cooking.
9. Remove the zeppoles from the Air Fryer and immediately dust them with powdered sugar.
10. Serve hot with optional chocolate sauce or raspberry jam for dipping.

Air Fryer Jerk Chicken Wings

Serves 2 / Prep Time: 15 minutes / Cook Time: 25 minutes

- For the Jerk Marinade:
- 20g jerk seasoning
- 10g olive oil
- 5g soy sauce
- 5g brown sugar
- 5g lime juice
- 2 cloves garlic, minced
- 400g chicken wings, separated and patted dry
- For the Jerk Dipping Sauce:
- 30g mayonnaise
- 10g jerk seasoning
- 5g lime juice

1. Preheat your Ninja Foodi Dual Zone Air Fryer to 375°F (190°C) on the "Air Fry" setting.
2. In a bowl, mix jerk seasoning, olive oil, soy sauce, brown sugar, lime juice, and minced garlic to create the jerk marinade.
3. Toss the chicken wings in the jerk marinade, ensuring they are well coated.
4. In a separate bowl, combine mayonnaise, jerk seasoning, and lime juice to make the jerk dipping sauce.
5. In one air fryer zone, place the marinated chicken wings.
6. Air fry at 375°F (190°C) for about 20-25 minutes, turning them once or twice during cooking, until the wings are crispy and cooked through.
7. Serve the jerk chicken wings with the jerk dipping sauce on the side.
8. Enjoy your Air Fryer Jerk Chicken Wings!

Ham and Cheese Croissant Bites

Serves 2 / Prep Time: 15 minutes / Cook Time: 10 minutes

- 2 mini croissants
- 50g ham, sliced
- 50g Swiss cheese, sliced
- 10g Dijon mustard
- 10g mayonnaise

1. Preheat your Ninja Foodi Dual Zone Air Fryer to 350°F (175°C) on the "Air Fry" setting.
2. Slice the mini croissants in half.
3. In a small bowl, mix the Dijon mustard and mayonnaise.
4. Spread the Dijon-mayo mixture on the cut sides of the croissants.
5. Layer the ham and Swiss cheese on the bottom halves of the croissants.
6. Place the croissant tops on the cheese and ham to form sandwiches.
7. Arrange the croissant bites in the air fryer basket.
8. Air fry at 350°F (175°C) for about 8-10 minutes, or until the croissants are golden and the cheese is melted.
9. Serve your Ham and Cheese Croissant Bites hot and enjoy this savory treat.

Mini Apple Hand Pies with Salted Caramel Drizzle

Serves 2 / Prep Time: 20 minutes / Cook Time: 12 minutes

- 2 mini pie crusts (about 150g each)
- 150g apples, peeled and diced
- 20g sugar
- 5g cinnamon

- 10g unsalted butter, melted
- 10g salted caramel sauce (plus extra for drizzling)
- 5g flour

1. Preheat your Ninja Foodi Dual Zone Air Fryer to 350°F (175°C) on the "Bake" setting.
2. In a bowl, mix the diced apples, sugar, cinnamon, melted butter, salted caramel sauce, and flour until the apples are coated.
3. Roll out the mini pie crusts and cut them into 4-inch circles.
4. Place a spoonful of the apple mixture onto one half of each pie crust circle.
5. Fold the other half over to create a semi-circle and seal the edges by pressing with a fork.
6. Place the hand pies in the air fryer basket.
7. Air fry at 350°F (175°C) for about 10-12 minutes, or until the pies are golden brown.
8. Drizzle with extra salted caramel sauce before serving.
9. Enjoy your Mini Apple Hand Pies with Salted Caramel Drizzle.

Air Fryer S'mores

Serves 2 / Prep Time: 5 minutes / Cook Time: 5 minutes

- 4 graham cracker sheets (2 full sheets, broken in half)
- 4 large marshmallows
- 40g milk chocolate, broken into small pieces

1. Break the graham cracker sheets in half to make 4 squares.
2. Preheat your Ninja Foodi Dual Zone Air Fryer to 350°F (180°C) on the "Roast" setting.
3. Place 2 graham cracker squares on the air fryer rack. Top each square with a marshmallow.
4. Insert the air fryer rack into the Ninja Foodi Dual Zone Air Fryer.
5. Air fry the marshmallow-topped graham crackers at 350°F (180°C) for 4-5 minutes, or until the marshmallows are golden brown and puffy.
6. Carefully remove the rack from the air fryer and place the chocolate pieces on top of the marshmallows.
7. Place the remaining graham cracker squares on top of the chocolate and press down gently to create the S'mores.
8. Return the rack to the air fryer for 1 more minute to allow the chocolate to melt slightly.
9. Remove the S'mores from the air fryer and let them cool for a moment before indulging.

Churros with Chocolate Sauce

Serves 2 / Prep Time: 20 minutes / Cook Time: 15 minutes

- For the Churros:
- 100g all-purpose flour
- 5g granulated sugar
- 2g salt
- 200ml water
- 30g unsalted butter
- 1 egg
- 2g vanilla extract
- 20g vegetable oil (for brushing)
- For the Chocolate Sauce:
- 100g dark chocolate, chopped
- 60ml heavy cream

1. Preheat your Ninja Foodi Dual Zone Air Fryer to 375°F (190°C) on the "Air Fry" setting.
2. In a saucepan, combine water, granulated sugar, salt, and unsalted butter. Bring to a boil.
3. Remove the saucepan from heat and stir in all-purpose flour until a dough forms.
4. Let the dough cool slightly, then beat in the egg and vanilla extract.
5. Transfer the dough to a piping bag with a star tip.
6. In a separate saucepan, heat heavy cream until it's hot but not boiling. Remove from heat and add chopped dark chocolate, stirring until smooth.
7. In one air fryer zone, pipe the churros onto a piece of parchment paper, then brush them with vegetable oil.
8. Air fry at 375°F (190°C) for about 10-15 minutes, or until the churros are golden brown.
9. In the other air fryer zone, place the saucepan with the chocolate sauce and reheat it if needed.
10. Serve your churros with warm chocolate sauce.
11. Enjoy your Churros with Chocolate Sauce!

chapter 9 Dessert

Fried Banana Spring Rolls with Nutella Dip

Serves 2 / Prep Time: 20 minutes / Cook Time: 10 minutes

- For the Banana Spring Rolls:
- 4 spring roll wrappers
- 2 ripe bananas, peeled and cut in half lengthwise
- 1/4 cup brown sugar (60g)
- 1/2 teaspoon ground cinnamon
- Vegetable oil for frying
- For the Nutella Dip:
- 1/4 cup Nutella (60g)
- 1 tablespoon heavy cream

1. In a small bowl, combine the brown sugar and ground cinnamon.
2. Lay out a spring roll wrapper with one corner pointing towards you. Place a banana half on the wrapper and sprinkle it with the brown sugar-cinnamon mixture.
3. Fold the sides of the wrapper in towards the center, then roll it up tightly, sealing the top corner with a bit of water to make a secure seal.
4. Repeat this process for the remaining wrappers and bananas.
5. Preheat your Ninja Foodi Dual Zone Air Fryer to 375°F (190°C).
6. Brush or spray the spring rolls with a little vegetable oil to help them crisp up in the air fryer.
7. Place the spring rolls in the air fryer basket.
8. Cook at 375°F (190°C) for about 8-10 minutes, turning halfway through, or until they are golden brown and crispy.

Air Fryer Mini Cheesecakes

Serves 2 / Prep Time: 15 minutes / Cook Time: 18 minutes

- For the Cheesecake:
- 200g cream cheese, softened
- 50g granulated sugar • 1 egg
- 5ml vanilla extract • 20g all-purpose flour
- 30ml sour cream
- For the Crust:
- 100g graham cracker crumbs
- 30g unsalted butter, melted
- Fresh berries or fruit compote for toppings

1. Preheat your Ninja Foodi Dual Zone Air Fryer to 325°F (160°C) on the "Air Fry" setting.
2. In a bowl, combine graham cracker crumbs with melted butter. Press the mixture into the bottom of two ramekins to create the crust.
3. In a separate bowl, beat the softened cream cheese until smooth. Add granulated sugar and mix until well combined.
4. Stir in the egg, vanilla extract, all-purpose flour, and sour cream until the cheesecake batter is smooth.
5. In one air fryer zone, place the ramekins with the crust.
6. Air fry at 325°F (160°C) for about 4-5 minutes to set the crust.
7. In the other air fryer zone, pour the cheesecake batter into the ramekins with the pre-cooked crusts.
8. Air fry at 325°F (160°C) for about 14-15 minutes, or until the cheesecakes are set but still slightly jiggly in the center.
9. Let them cool and refrigerate for a few hours or until they're completely chilled.
10. Top with fresh berries or fruit compote if desired.
11. Enjoy your Air Fryer Mini Cheesecakes!

Air Fryer Apple Fritters

Serves 2 / Prep Time: 15 minutes / Cook Time: 10 minutes

- For the Fritters:
- 100g all-purpose flour • 20g granulated sugar
- 5g baking powder • A pinch of salt
- 60ml milk • 1 egg
- 5ml vanilla extract
- 2 apples, peeled, cored, and diced
- Vegetable oil (for brushing)
- For the Glaze:
- 60g powdered sugar
- 10ml milk
- 2ml vanilla extract

1. Preheat your Ninja Foodi Dual Zone Air Fryer to 375°F (190°C) on the "Air Fry" setting.
2. In a bowl, mix all-purpose flour, granulated sugar, baking powder, and a pinch of salt.
3. In another bowl, whisk together milk, egg, and vanilla extract.
4. Combine the wet and dry ingredients until you have a smooth batter.
5. Gently fold in the diced apples.

6. In one air fryer zone, drop spoonfuls of the apple fritter batter onto a piece of parchment paper, forming fritter shapes.
7. Air fry at 375°F (190°C) for about 8-10 minutes, or until the fritters are golden brown and cooked through.
8. In the other air fryer zone, mix powdered sugar, milk, and vanilla extract to create the glaze.
9. Drizzle the glaze over the warm apple fritters.
10. Enjoy your Air Fryer Apple Fritters!

Funnel Cakes

Serves 2 / Prep Time: 10 minutes / Cook Time: 10 minutes

- 100g all-purpose flour
- 2g baking powder
- 2g salt
- 15g granulated sugar
- 1 egg
- 120ml milk
- 2ml vanilla extract
- Vegetable oil (for brushing)
- Powdered sugar (for dusting)

1. Preheat your Ninja Foodi Dual Zone Air Fryer to 375°F (190°C) on the "Air Fry" setting.
2. In a bowl, whisk together all-purpose flour, baking powder, salt, and granulated sugar.
3. In another bowl, beat the egg and then add milk and vanilla extract.
4. Combine the wet and dry ingredients until you have a smooth batter.
5. In one air fryer zone, use a funnel or a plastic squeeze bottle with a small hole to pour the batter in a circular, crisscross pattern to create the funnel cakes.
6. Air fry at 375°F (190°C) for about 5 minutes on each side, or until they are golden brown.
7. In the other air fryer zone, brush the funnel cakes with a little vegetable oil to help crisp them up.
8. Dust with powdered sugar while they're still warm.
9. Enjoy your Funnel Cakes!

Air Fryer Brownies

Serves 2 / Prep Time: 10 minutes / Cook Time: 20 minutes

- 50g unsalted butter
- 80g granulated sugar
- 25g cocoa powder
- 1 egg
- 2ml vanilla extract
- 35g all-purpose flour
- 1g salt

1. Preheat your Ninja Foodi Dual Zone Air Fryer to 325°F (160°C) on the "Air Fry" setting.
2. In a microwave-safe bowl, melt the unsalted butter.
3. Stir in granulated sugar and cocoa powder until well combined.
4. Beat in the egg and vanilla extract.
5. Gradually add all-purpose flour and a pinch of salt, mixing until smooth.
6. In one air fryer zone, pour the brownie batter into a greased and lined pan.
7. Air fry at 325°F (160°C) for about 18-20 minutes, or until a toothpick comes out with a few moist crumbs.
8. Let the brownies cool before cutting into squares.
9. Enjoy your Air Fryer Brownies!

Air Fryer Cinnamon Rolls

Serves 2 / Prep Time: 10 minutes / Cook Time: 12 minutes

- 1 sheet of pre-made cinnamon roll dough
- Icing (included with the dough)

1. Preheat your Ninja Foodi Dual Zone Air Fryer to 350°F (175°C) on the "Air Fry" setting.
2. Unroll the pre-made cinnamon roll dough.
3. Cut the dough in half, creating two portions.
4. In one air fryer zone, place the cinnamon roll portions.
5. Air fry at 350°F (175°C) for about 10-12 minutes, or until they are golden brown and cooked through.
6. In the other air fryer zone, warm the icing briefly in a microwave to make it easier to drizzle.
7. Drizzle the warm cinnamon rolls with the included icing.
8. Enjoy your Air Fryer Cinnamon Rolls!

Air Fryer Blueberry Muffins

Serves 2 / Prep Time: 15 minutes / Cook Time: 15 minutes

- 120g all-purpose flour
- 30g granulated sugar
- 5g baking powder
- 2.5g baking soda
- 2.5g salt
- 60g unsalted butter, melted
- 1 large egg
- 120ml buttermilk
- 60g blueberries (fresh or frozen)

1. In a mixing bowl, combine the all-purpose flour, granulated sugar, baking powder, baking soda, and salt. Mix well.
2. In a separate bowl, whisk together the melted unsalted butter, egg, and buttermilk until well combined.
3. Pour the wet ingredients into the dry ingredients and stir until just combined. Be careful not to overmix; a few lumps are okay.
4. Gently fold in the blueberries..
5. Preheat your Ninja Foodi Dual Zone Air Fryer to 350°F (180°C) on the "Bake" setting.
6. While the air fryer is preheating, line the air fryer basket or muffin cups with liners. If using a basket,

you can place silicone muffin cups in it.
7. Divide the muffin batter evenly between two muffin cups.
8. Place the muffin cups into the air fryer basket.
9. Insert the air fryer basket into the Ninja Foodi Dual Zone Air Fryer.
10. Air fry the blueberry muffins at 350°F (180°C) for 12-15 minutes, or until a toothpick inserted into the center of a muffin comes out clean.
11. Once done, remove the muffins from the air fryer and let them cool for a few minutes.
12. Serve warm and enjoy your delicious air fryer blueberry muffins.

Blueberry Lemon Cornmeal Muffins

Serves 2 / Prep Time: 15 minutes / Cook Time: 20 minutes

- 100g all-purpose flour
- 50g cornmeal
- 10g baking powder
- 5g baking soda
- 3g salt
- 60g sugar
- Zest of 1 lemon
- 100g unsalted butter, melted and cooled
- 2 large eggs
- 150g buttermilk
- 100g fresh blueberries

1. Preheat your Ninja Foodi Dual Zone Air Fryer to 350°F (175°C) on the "Bake" setting.
2. In a bowl, whisk together the all-purpose flour, cornmeal, baking powder, baking soda, salt, sugar, and lemon zest.
3. In a separate bowl, whisk the melted butter, eggs, and buttermilk until well combined.
4. Gently fold the wet ingredients into the dry ingredients until just combined.
5. Gently fold in the fresh blueberries.
6. Line a muffin tin with paper liners.
7. Fill each liner about 2/3 full with the muffin batter.
8. Place the muffin tin in the air fryer basket and bake at 350°F (175°C) for about 18-20 minutes, or until a toothpick inserted into the center of a muffin comes out clean.
9. Remove the muffins from the air fryer and let them cool before serving.
10. Enjoy your Blueberry Lemon Cornmeal Muffins.

Air Fryer Chocolate-Dipped Coconut Macaroons

Serves 2 / Prep Time: 15 minutes / Cook Time: 12 minutes

- 100g sweetened shredded coconut
- 50g sweetened condensed milk
- 5g vanilla extract
- 100g semi-sweet chocolate chips
- 10g coconut oil

1. Preheat your Ninja Foodi Dual Zone Air Fryer to 325°F (160°C) on the "Air Fry" setting.
2. In a bowl, mix the sweetened shredded coconut, sweetened condensed milk, and vanilla extract until well combined.
3. Shape the coconut mixture into small macaroon-sized balls and place them on a parchment paper-lined tray.
4. Place the tray in the air fryer and air fry at 325°F (160°C) for about 10-12 minutes, or until the macaroons are golden brown.
5. While the macaroons cool, melt the semi-sweet chocolate chips and coconut oil together.
6. Dip each macaroon into the melted chocolate mixture, allowing any excess to drip off.
7. Place the chocolate-dipped macaroons on a tray lined with parchment paper.
8. Allow the chocolate to set.
9. Enjoy your Air Fryer Chocolate-Dipped Coconut Macaroons.

Air Fryer Chocolate Chip Cookies

Serves 2 / Prep Time: 15 minutes / Cook Time: 10 minutes

- 100g all-purpose flour
- 2g baking soda
- 2g salt
- 60g unsalted butter, melted
- 50g brown sugar
- 40g granulated sugar
- 1 egg
- 5g vanilla extract
- 100g chocolate chips

1. Preheat your Ninja Foodi Dual Zone Air Fryer to 350°F (175°C) on the "Air Fry" setting.
2. In a bowl, mix all-purpose flour, baking soda, and salt.
3. In another bowl, whisk together melted unsalted butter, brown sugar, granulated sugar, egg, and vanilla extract.
4. Gradually add the dry ingredients to the wet ingredients, mixing until just combined.
5. Stir in the chocolate chips.
6. Scoop cookie dough and form it into two equal-sized cookie balls.
7. In one air fryer zone, place the cookie dough balls.
8. Air fry at 350°F (175°C) for about 8-10 minutes, or until the cookies are golden and slightly soft in the center.
9. Let them cool for a few minutes before serving.
10. Enjoy your Air Fryer Chocolate Chip Cookies!

Printed in Great Britain
by Amazon